A SPIRITUAL GUIDE THROUGH *ANXIETY*

A Companion Guide for

ANXIETY, PHOBIAS & PANIC:
Taking Charge and Conquering Fear

Marjorie Working

Copyright © 1990 by Marjorie Working

All rights reserved. No part of this book may be reproduced in any form or by any means, electronic or mechanical, including photocopy, recording, in the form of a phonographic recording, or any information storage and retrieval system, without permission in writing from the publisher except in the case of brief quotations embodied in critical articles and reviews. The circumstances of certain events depicted and the names of individuals have been altered and/or deleted to protect the privacy of the people involved.

Library of Congress in Publication Data

Working, Marjorie, 1936-
    A spiritual guide through anxiety: a supplement to Anxiety, phobias & panic/ by Marjorie Working.
        p. cm.
    Includes bibliographical references.
    ISBN 0-929437-12-8: $6.95
    1. Anxiety--Religious aspects--Christianity.   2. Christian life--1960-   I. Peurifoy, Reneau Z. Anxiety, phobias & panic. II. Title.
BF575.A6945   1988 Suppl.
248.8'6--dc20
                                                              89-36842
                                                                  CIP

Printed in the United States of America, First printing January, 1990

10 9 8 7 6 5 4 3 2 1

Contents

	Page
Foreword	ii
Acknowledgements	iii
Getting Started	iv
Spiritual Path To Freedom	vi
Supplement to Lesson 1: Why Me?	1
Supplement to Lesson 2: Making Peace With Your Fleshly Nature	5
Supplement to Lesson 3: The Importance of Re-Creation	9
Supplement to Lesson 4: Renewing Your Mind	15
Supplement to Lesson 5: Gaining A Spiritual Perspective	19
Supplement to Lesson 6: Adequate Servanthood	25
Supplement to Lesson 7: Cast Your Burdens On The Lord	29
Supplement to Lesson 8: As One Approved	33
Supplement to Lesson 9: Reconnecting With The Body of Christ	39
Supplement to Lesson 10: Transformation	43
Supplement to Lesson 11: Celebrating God's Work In You	47
Supplement to Lesson 12: Anger—God's Confusing Gift	51
Supplement to Lesson 13: Power Under Control	55
Supplement to Lesson 14: Remember Whose You Are	59
Supplement to Lesson 15: Continuing Your Growth	63
Recommended Reading	65
Index	67
Listing of Bible Verses	68
Supplemental Materials	69

Foreword

When I first began to plan the writing of *Anxiety, Phobias & Panic* I knew that I would want a book such as this *Spiritual Guide* to eventually be available for Christians facing anxiety-related problems. There are two reasons for this. First, Christians facing anxiety-related problems often create additional, unnecessary stress and anxiety for themselves because of misunderstandings of what it is to be a Christian. Second, a person's problems cannot be arbitrarily separated from the spiritual side of that person's life. Unfortunately, modern psychology often tries to do just that and work with people in a spiritual vacuum.

I met Marjorie Working when I joined a small group at my church that she was leading. After a few Sunday's I knew that the Lord had sent her into my life and approached her with the idea of writing this book. While it was quite a process to actually complete the book, I felt that every step of the way was under His guidance. The result is a work that I am sure will enable many to not only overcome their anxiety-related problems, but will also bring those who follow the suggestions it makes closer to God. It has certainly deepened my spiritual insight and made a profound impact on how I approach life.

Reneau Z. Peurifoy, M.A., M.F.C.C.
author of *Anxiety, Phobias & Panic*

Acknowledgements

Only the Lord, working through a patient person like Reneau Peurifoy, who oversaw this project, could have continued to exhort and encourage me as this book came about. I gratefully acknowledge my thanks and dependence on them in this endeavor.

Paula and Ron Wessels allowed me to camp in their family room and gave me a crash course in the use of the computer/word processor. Without complaint, both of them, along with Cliff Graves, another friend at Christ Community Church, answered countless questions and retrieved lost chapters for me.

Others helped by reading and offering valuable suggestions for improving my manuscript. They were Mark Lau Banson, Alissyn Link, Karen Read, Cheri Smith, Joan Mathison, Joan Werkhoven, Russel Working, Michiyo Peurifoy, Nina Lau-Branson, Ken Stabler, Dee Green, and Dave Pascoa.

Courageous friends trustingly confided their process in overcoming anxiety, phobias, and panic. Their input about how Christ has sustained them both instructed and inspired me.

I am grateful to the fellow pilgrims on the path of spirituality from the class my husband and I taught this spring at the San Francisco Extension of Fuller Theological Seminary. They showed me much about the riches to be found in the lives and writings of Christian seekers in all the ages and traditions of the church. I thank them for opening their journals and hearts to witness to the faithfulness of the Lord Jesus Christ.

My family always emboldens me to accept new challenges, and this book was another opportunity for me to appreciate their support.

This is dedicated to my husband, Kenneth, who is in everything of value I do. He is the one who taught me that my other name is "Beloved."

GETTING STARTED

We have a great Shepherd, Jesus Christ, Who is our Guide over life's uneven paths. This book is a companion to Reneau Z. Peurifoy's *Anxiety, Phobias & Panic: Taking charge and conquering Fear*. It adds biblical principles and a review of the scriptures which deal with claiming God's peace to the program you have begun. This is meant to be more than a review of the Bible's promises. Hopefully it will invoke the presence of the Lord Who makes and keeps promises. Through it, I pray that you will rejoice not only because of your victory over the problems that bring you to this program, but that increasingly you will rejoice in the Lord Himself.

> Rejoice in the Lord always. I will say it again: Rejoice! Let your gentleness be evident to all. The Lord is near. Do not be anxious about anything, but in everything, by prayer and petition, with thanksgiving, present your requests to God. And the peace of God, which transcends all understanding, will guard your hearts and your minds in Christ Jesus (Philippians 4:4-7).

You may have been told many times, "Don't be anxious," and felt guilt over not being a serene and imperturbable child of God. Sometimes you may even wonder if you are a Christian at all if you lack the trust and discipline to overcome your fears. But the Bible teaches that our salvation is not determined by our worthiness, but by Christ's. We are considered God's children because we believe and receive Jesus Christ as Savior and Lord. Our eternal destiny is determined by what He did for us on the cross. Jesus' resurrection power is yours when you commit your life to Him and determine to live a holy life by the power of His Spirit.

As you begin this program, see it as part of God's process for changing your life. Give it the time, the patience, and (here's an idea we don't much like) *submission* it requires.

> Humble yourselves, therefore, under God's mighty hand, that He may lift you up in due time. Cast all your anxiety on Him because He cares for you. Be self-controlled and alert...And the God of all grace, who called you to His eternal glory in Christ, after you have suffered a little while, will Himself restore you and make you strong, firm, and steadfast (1 Peter 5:6-8a, 10).

Circle the words in the above passage that indicate this is a process over a period of time. Often we demand instant results and magic deliverance and instead He offers to be our Companion on the way for as long as it takes.

How to Proceed

Each week read the lesson in *Anxiety, Phobias & Panic* on which you are working. Then do the corresponding lesson in this book, combining it with a time of solitude with the Lord.

Find a quiet corner where you won't be disturbed. Try to regulate the time several days a week so that mediation on God's Word, prayer, and reflecting on these in a prayer journal become habitual. Your journal can be a simple spiral notebook or an elaborate covered book sold in stationery or book stores. Keeping a journal will allow you to review your progress.

Start by singing or reading a hymn. Use the breathing and other relaxation techniques found on pages 37-38 of *Anxiety, Phobias & Panic* and purposefully enter into the peace of God. Meditate on His Word. There are many reasons and ways to read the Bible: "All Scripture is inspired by God and profitable for teaching, for reproof, for correction, for training in righteousness" (2 Timothy 3:16).

For our purposes here, we suggest taking only a few verses to read meditatively; that is, in a way that you ponder the meaning for your own life. In doing so, recognize that "the Word of God is living and active. Sharper than any double-edged sword, it penetrates even to dividing soul and spirit, joints and marrow; it judges thoughts and attitudes of the heart" (Hebrews 4:12). When you meditate on the Word, *it* reads *you*.

Use the verses from each lesson for your meditation. You may want to copy them on cards you can carry with you to memorize. This can be a powerful way to remind yourself of God's presence and can be used as a distraction when anxiety threatens your tranquility.

Over the ages, believers have valued prayer partners, spiritual guides or spiritual friends to accompany them on their faith journey. Choose a support person for this program who will pray with and for you. Look for someone who is mature in faith, accepting of others' differences and wants to grow also. Have more than one possible support person in mind and don't let disappointment keep you from asking another if your first choice is too busy or unable to work with you. Pray that the Lord will find the right person for you.

A Word About Spiritual Warfare

Sometimes Christians believe that their anxiety symptoms indicate demonic activity. While this is possible—the Enemy can use any weakness or infirmity to discourage us— it is seldom the case in our culture. If these worries persist after studying the usual causes of anxiety problems found in lesson one of *Anxiety, Phobias & Panic*, or you are troubled by obsessive-compulsive behaviors involving religious rituals to keep demons at bay or remove demonic contamination, talk to your pastor. As believers are inhabited by the Holy Spirit, Christians needn't be concerned about demon possession. We need to remember that Christ prays that we will be kept from the evil one (John 17:15). Paul describes the Christian's defense against the devil in Ephesians 6:11-18. James 4:7 says, "Submit...to God. Resist the devil and he will flee from you."

A CHRISTIAN'S PATH TO FREEDOM

by Reneau Z. Peurifoy
amplified by Marjorie Working

As each day passes,

I am better able to embrace and love myself and others, knowing that God chose to create each of us;

I am better able to understand that feelings are part of that person God intended me to be, and knowing this, allow them to flow freely through me;

I am better able to think rationally and realistically, to look at life as a series of choices that God wants me to make as one created in His image with free will, and to stop and look before choosing;

I am better able to know that perfection exists only in Jesus Christ, and for me it is a direction rather than a place. Therefore, I am better able to confess my sins and move on, free to laugh at my human mistakes and imperfections;

I am better able to trust the Lord for my transformation into that person He intends me to become; patient with time, facing my world with courage, knowing that in Him, each day I take another step on the Path to Freedom.

Supplement to

1

Lesson

Why Me?

Psalm 139
(Selected Verses)

O Lord, Thou hast searched me and known me.
Thou dost know when I sit down and when I rise up;
Thou dost understand my thought from afar.
Thou dost scrutinize my path and my lying down,
And art intimately acquainted with all my ways.
Even before there is a word on my tongue,
Behold, O Lord, Thou dost know it all.
Thou hast enclosed me behind and before,
And laid Thy hand upon me.
Such knowledge is too wonderful for me;
It is too high, I cannot attain to it...
For Thou didst form my inward parts;
Thou didst weave me in my mother's womb.
I will give thanks to Thee, for I am fearfully and wonderfully made.

Wonderful are Thy works,
And my soul knows it very well.
My frame was not hidden from Thee,
When I was made in secret,
And skillfully wrought in the depths of the earth.
Thine eyes have seen my unformed substance...
Search me, O God, and know my heart;
Try me and know my anxious thoughts;
And see if there be any hurtful way in me,
And lead me in the everlasting way."

"We human beings are the height of God's creation," Dr. Kenneth Working, a pastor, said in a recent sermon. "Physically, we have a skeletal structure of some 106 bones, manipulated by a muscular system of over 600 muscles. They enable us to run and bend and jump. We have a life pump called the heart that sends blood to a circulatory system that if stretched it would reach more than 60,000 miles.

"To operate all of this, God gave us a nervous system made of the brain, the spinal cord and a complex of nerves that can send impulses over 350 feet per second. Add to this a digestive and elimination system for refueling, and a marvelous reproductive system. We are truly 'fearfully and wonderfully made'!"

Believers struggling with anxiety often ask, "Why has God allowed me to suffer this? Is my failure to overcome my fears actually a lack of trust in God? Is all of this a punishment for sin, or perhaps a sign that I really have no faith in the Lord?"

Even though you may be able to agree in general that the human body is wonderfully made, you may suspect that God has abandoned you and your particular body to the miseries of anxiety-related problems.

The problem of pain and the function of it in a world created by a loving God is one that has puzzled many. But encouragement for such a program as this, and for not simply accepting your anxiety problems as "just the way I am," begins in the opening chapters of the Bible, Genesis 1-3. Here, we are told that we are the intentional creation of a loving God who made us to be like Him and to be with Him: "So God created man in His own image, in the image of God He created him; male and female He created them" (Genesis 1:27). Besides bearing His image, He gave us dominion to rule "over every living thing that moves on the earth." Presumably, since we too are among the living things that move on the earth, this rule includes us with our emotions, actions, and habits. God provides responsibility, tasks, and companionship indicating that we can make powerful choices about how we deal with life.

Someone might object that a quick look around reveals that our dominion is certainly not apparent. Everywhere we see evidence that something other than God's

Supplement to Lesson 1: Why Me?

image-bearers are at work on the planet. Death, disease, disorder in the form of pollution, war, and crime seem to rule the lives of the sons and daughters of Adam and Eve.

Genesis 3 tells both the bad news and the good news regarding this plight. Verses 1-3 tell of the serpent, called in other passages Satan, the devil (Revelation 12:9), the father of lies (John 8:44), the prince of this world (John 14:30), and the god of this age (2 Corinthians 4:4). This serpent instigated a rebellion against God that has affected and been repeated by all men and women since. Every facet of life is impacted, as we can see in the verses that follow (Genesis 3:3-24). Our common parents found that the natural intimacy with God, with one another, and with their own bodies and purpose in life was broken. It is bad news indeed to reflect that because of the Fall, each of us experiences sin and the effects of living in a world filled with brokenness and disease (*dis-ease*) of all sorts.

Yet the bad news is not the final news. Even as the rebellion against Him took place, God had a plan for restoring us to Himself. Verse 15 foretells a child to be born of woman who will "crush the head of the serpent" even as the serpent "bruises his heel." This Child is, of course, Jesus Christ, whose heel was bruised on the cross as He died to redeem us from this tyrant and the effects of the Fall in our lives.

Though he has been dealt the death blow, the tail of the serpent still thrashes, causing havoc among the just as well as the unjust. People still walk through pain, disease and death in this life. But just as our Savior Jesus Christ repealed the death sentence by taking it upon Himself on our behalf at Calvary, He offers eternal life to all.

Now, we know that eternal life is not just "fire insurance" that keeps us out of hell and admits us to heaven at some vague future time. It is also a quality of life to enjoy now and for all time. "I have come that they might have life, and have it to the full (or abundantly)" (John 10:10). This life is for all. Jesus said that He "must be lifted up (crucified); that everyone who believes in Him may have eternal life." (John 3:14, 15). As we shall see, one purpose for our life between discovering this astonishing fact and His return is to claim, make our own, the abundant life that Jesus came to give us. It is a process which we continue until that day when He returns to establish a new heaven and a new earth.

Now the dwelling of God is with men, and He will live with them. They will be His people, and God Himself will be with them and be their God. He will wipe every tear from their eyes. There will be no more death or mourning or crying or pain, for the old order of things has passed away (Revelation 21:3, 4).

In creation God gave us His image; in the Fall we and the world around us became broken, and in bondage to death. In redemption we are bought back by Jesus' death and we begin a life-long journey of being made whole and holy.

Recommended Activities

Unleash the Power of Scripture and Prayer

Here are four ways in which you can begin to unleash the power of Scripture and prayer.

- Read Psalm 139 and Revelation 21:3, 4 on pages 1 and 3 each day as you work with this lesson. You may want to memorize all or part of these verses or copy them onto a card you can put on your mirror or elsewhere.

- Use Psalm 139 in this lesson as a prayer. Insert your name in the appropriate spots as you read it aloud. Underline those passages that you find helpful.

- Thank the Lord for including you as part of His good creation.

- Thank God that He is still the Creator and wants you to join Him as He continues the process of helping you become that person He intends you to be.

Find a Study Partner and/or Support Group

Find someone to support you spiritually. Choose a person you trust to learn along with you. Select someone who will agree to pray with you each time you meet for the specific goals and skills you are working on, perhaps using the review for each lesson which starts on page 220 of *Anxiety, Phobias & Panic*. Or, you may decide to read aloud together each new lesson you begin. Also commit to pray daily for one another between your meetings.

Ask God to Help You Reduce Stress

Alone or with your support person or group, examine before the Lord activities or situations that may be causing stress. If the pressure and stress you are experiencing comes from ministry or church involvements, it might even be possible that the Lord wants you to take a break from these while you are working with Him on your anxiety problems.

Remember, you are made in God's image to have dominion over everything that moves on the earth. He loves you and created you for Himself. Through Jesus, God gives you full, abundant and eternal life. He wants you to be alert and self-controlled, casting your anxiety on Him. He will be with you throughout, and will Himself restore you and make you strong, firm and steadfast (1 Peter 5:6-10). However, He waits for and wants your cooperation in this process.

Making Peace With Your Fleshly Nature

Supplement to Lesson 2

Notice that the title of Lesson 2 in *Anxiety, Phobias & Panic* is *not* "Eliminating Stress from Your Life." Stress is part of life. As we recognized in the last lesson, we live on a fallen planet where all humans experience a share of conflict, brokenness and hurt. This will be true until the Lord returns.

You may assume that anyone, even the faithful saints, can have the flu, broken bones or heart attacks, but only the "spiritual weakling" suffers from anxiety. When trying to answer the big "Why me?", you might even think such things as, "I must be pretty marginal in God's scheme if He allows me this condition. I must be a real Christian wimp when things get me down to the extent that it effects my body!".

If so, consider these words of the apostle Paul: "For even when we came into Macedonia, this body of ours had no rest, but we were harassed at every turn—conflicts on the outside, fears within. But God, who comforts the downcast, comforted us by the coming of Titus" (2 Corinthians 7:5, 6). And this was written by one who was picked by God to fill out the ranks of the apostles and to write more than a fourth of the New Testament.

Perhaps even more poignant is the description of his struggle with self-control in Romans 7:15-25. Though Paul is referring to the battle between the law and sin in his life, it also captures the difficulty of overcoming the habits of anxiety and compulsions.

> I cannot understand my own behavior. I fail to carry out the things I want to do, and I find myself doing the very things I hate. When I act against my own will, that means I have a self that acknowledges that the law is good, and so the thing behaving in that way is not my self but sin living in me. The fact is, I know nothing good living in me...for though the will to do what is good is in me, the performance is not, with the result that instead of doing the good things I want to do, I carry out the sinful things I do not want...I can see that my body follows a different law that battles against the law which my reason dictates...What a wretched man I am! Who will rescue me from this body doomed to death: Thanks be to God through Jesus Christ our Lord! (Romans 7:15-25, Jerusalem Bible)

Like most Christians, Paul is aware that he is stuck with a body in which the spiritual nature is at war with the human or *fleshly* nature. Yet, this is not a war where the outcome is unknown. Paul, even in the midst of his struggle and frustration, thanks his Champion Christ Jesus who has already won the war. Paul enlists himself and all of us who look to the Word for help to resist the temptation to give in to despair and "just-the-way-I-am-ness":

> What shall we say, then? Shall we go on sinning (or accepting our anxiety problems as permanent) so that grace may increase? By no means! We died to sin; how can we live in it any longer? Or don't you know that all of us who were baptized into his death...in order that, just as Christ was raised from the dead through the glory of the Father, we too may live a new life? (Romans 6:1-4).

In the same way, you may be "stuck with" a sensitive body, a tendency to hyperventilate, and a high anxiety personality. However, this does not mean that anxiety or fear have to rule your life. "(You) too may live a new life" (Romans 6:4).

In order to live this new life you need to understand certain things about yourself. First and foremost, *you are not God.* While you are created in God's image, a reflection of His character, you can never outgrow the need for a relationship and a reliance on God. Adam and Eve got into trouble when they succumbed to the temptation to exchange bearing the image of God for acting as gods in their own lives. They forgot their creatureliness. When we remember ours, we are able to accept the limitations which are part of any creature's life, and we are able to make use of the resources that our loving Creator provides for us. This means that while we recognize that God is in control, we accept responsibility where He has delegated it to us.

Reneau Peurifoy's prescription to regard your body as a machine with a limited supply of energy that needs to be cared for regularly in order for it to work well, fits well with this biblical view of human responsibility. Our bodies need the right kind of fuel (diet) and maintenance (exercise and rest). They come with warning lights that tell us when they are overworked or overstressed. We all must learn how to read our own physical, mental, emotional, and spiritual fatigue symptoms.

Recommended Activities

Unleash the Power of Scripture and Prayer

Study the scriptures from this lesson, asking the Lord to show you how they apply to your life and this program you are doing.

Do a Body Maintenance Check

List the activities of an ordinary day in your life. Then list your activities in an ordinary week. Is there a rhythm of rest, work, and fun included? Write yourself a letter about how you are taking care of your body in regards to diet, exercise, and rest.

Write Your Own Version of the 23rd Psalm

Write your own version of the 23rd Psalm. Prayerfully substitute phrases that address your own situation as you speak to the Lord about the way He shows you He cares for you.

Supplement to Lesson 3

The Importance of Re-Creation

Here are some ways in which you can use spiritual principles to make your nine symptom-reducing approaches more powerful.

Coping Self-Statements

Negative self-talk in the Bible isn't left as the final word or an acceptable excuse for avoiding all uncomfortable situations. Jeremiah, the Old Testament prophet, recalls how the Lord corrected his first negative, self-denigrating response when called to be God's spokesman. (Who wouldn't be a little anxious?)

> I said, "alas, Lord God! I do not know how to for I am a youth.' But the Lord said to me, 'Do not say, I am a youth,' because everywhere I send you, you shall go, and all that I command you, you shall speak. Do not be afraid of them, for I am with you to deliver you..." (Jeremiah 1:6-8).

In the Psalms, David says that God put a "new song" in his mouth. Think of the new coping language you are learning as a new song you can "sing" as you approach, go through, and later evaluate difficult situations. Ask and expect God to give you a new song about yourself just as He did for David. Following are some examples of "new song" coping sentences.

Statements used when preparing for a stressful situation

"The Lord uses things like this in my life to help me grow. I wonder what He will teach me?"

"God has given me the skills I'm learning as resources. Which ones will be useful here?"

"Jesus promised to be with us to the end of the age. That includes being with me as I face this."

Statements used when confronting and handling a stressful situation

"The Lord has gotten me through tougher things than this in the past. He'll get me through this."

"My walk in faith is not 'an elimination game.' He will never leave nor forsake me, even if I don't do this perfectly. Besides, Christ is my perfection."

"There is no need to rush. Because of Jesus, I have all of eternity to change and grow. There are plenty of chances to keep trying this until I accomplish it."

"Lord, clear my mind and help me to concentrate on what needs to be done now."

"With God's help I can do all things necessary to become the person He wants me to be."

Statements used to cope with the feeling of being overwhelmed

"I am safe in God's ever-lasting arms. Though what I am feeling now is uncomfortable, it has no power to separate me from His love. This, too, will pass away."

"Remember, God is at work within me, both to will and to work for His good pleasure. As I let Him, He will bring glory to Himself even in this situation."

"Check your breathing. Use your diaphragm to breathe in God's Spirit, letting Him fill your whole being. Breathe out your anxieties and cares, casting them upon Him."

"He will not allow me to be tempted beyond what I can bear, but will in all ways provide a means for coping with what I am facing."

Reinforcing self-statements

"I did it! I can do all things through Him who strengthens me."

"I *am* being transformed. I know now I *can* change old habits or patterns. I did it once, I can do it again."

"Wait until I tell my support group (or person) about how the Lord was there with me!"

"His Word is reliable. He is my ever-present help!"

Supplement to Lesson 3: The Importance of Re-Creation

Distraction

Recalling memorized Bible verses provides you with both a powerful form of distraction as well as a powerful form of coping self-statements. Bible book stores often carry Bible promise cards which are easy to carry in your pocket or purse. You can make your own. Cards like these are good aids for memorizing scripture and for recalling the kinds of thoughts the Lord wants to fill your mind.

> Whatever is true, whatever is honorable, whatever is right, whatever is of good repute, if there is any excellence and if anything worthy of praise, let your mind dwell on these things (Philippians 4:8).

Did you know that these instructions are followed by a promise? "The things you have learned and received and heard and seen in me," says Paul, "practice these things; and the God of peace shall be with you."

Notice it says, "*practice* these things." It is in the rehearsing of what we have learned and received in God's Word that we experience His peace in our daily lives. Habitual behavior comes through repetition. Skills are valuable only if you *use* them.

Sabbath Keeping

Lesson 3 suggests other symptom-reducing approaches: relaxation, play, humor, emotional support, spiritual support, incorporating traditions and routines into your life. Intentional sabbath keeping provides the center where these approaches might become integrated in busy lives in which they might otherwise be neglected.

The Fourth Commandment says:

> Remember the sabbath day, to keep it holy. Six days you shall labor and do all your work, but the seventh day is a sabbath of the Lord your God; in it you shall not do any work... (Exodus 20:8-10).

While few believers would suggest that the remainder of the Ten Commandments are obsolete, the idea of resting for an entire day once a week may seem on the one hand self-indulgent or on the other hand an out-of-date practice by those who try to gain God's favor through self-denial. What does this forced inactivity that parents or grandparents remember with little fondness have to do with the grace and freedom we find in Jesus Christ? We are reminded of the privilege and provision of the sabbath when we look at what the Bible says about why God instituted it. The New Testament sees sabbath rest as a metaphor for the peace of God one experiences in Christ Jesus.

The Bible gives two reasons for keeping this day of rest or *repose* (for that is what sabbath means in Hebrew). First, God Himself rested on the seventh day after the work of creation. "(He) rested on the seventh day; therefore the Lord blessed the sabbath day and made it holy" (Exodus 20:11). *Holy* means to be set apart from the secular, the mundane, the ordinary, to the sacred. So, we follow God's own example. If *He* rested on the sabbath, how much more do we frail humans need to do the same each week?

Second, it is so that we may reflect on the spiritual heritage we have as God's chosen and now freed people:

Remember that you were slaves in Egypt and the Lord your God brought you out of there with a mighty hand and an outstretched arm. Therefore the Lord your God has commanded you to observe the sabbath (Deuteronomy 5:15).

One might protest, "What does legalism have to do with those who are free in Christ? Aren't we past keeping all the old laws?" True, the ceremonial laws of Israel, including those having to do with Temple worship and the food prohibitions, were replaced with the coming of the Holy Spirit and the extension of the Kingdom to include those previously separated by the temple walls. We understand those laws to have been preparation for the work of God in Christ Jesus. But His laws concerning love of God, neighbor, and self do not change; in fact, they are extended to include love of one's enemies.

Neither does law regarding the sabbath change. As the fourth of the Ten commandments, it stands as the pivot point between the first three which deal with how we are to worship (love) God and no other, and the final six which have to do with loving our neighbors. Keeping the sabbath enables us observe both sets of the commandments to love. The New Testament people in no way saw themselves as free from keeping the sabbath. Instead, they saw the sabbath infused with new meaning.

Hebrews 4:9-10 says, "There remains therefore a Sabbath rest for the people of God. For the one who has entered His rest has himself also rested from his works, as God did from His." Here, *sabbath rest* is a metaphor for both the Kingdom of God and for that inner state of spiritual security known as "salvation." So, for us who live on the resurrection side of the cross, sabbath rest has to do with our understanding that in Jesus, all the requirements of the law have been fulfilled. We can rest in Him, knowing that we are spiritually justified before the Father. Nothing needs to be added to the work of Christ's death on our behalf.

Still, the New Testament community took the first day of the week as a day of rest and remembering. Just as God contemplated His finished work of *creation*, we are called to contemplate His finished work of *redemption* in raising our Lord Jesus from the dead. In Christ we may enter into rest, and cease striving after "moral improvement" as a means of gaining God's favor. We know that Jesus bought our pardon and

Supplement to Lesson 3: The Importance of Re-Creation 13

righteousness for us on the cross. Our ministry or work as Christians is done not to gain God's approval, but out of a sense of gratitude and partnership with God in His kingdom.

Consider the benefits of keeping the sabbath for followers of Christ today in light of this lesson's symptom-reducing approaches. Contemplating God's work as we attend services of worship binds us with other believers and gives us a base from which to draw emotional and spiritual help. The reading of the Word, the sermon, the hymns, and the testimonies remind us of our "creatureliness" even while we acknowledge that we are made in God's image. As part of a *fallen* creation, we know that we are not perfect nor are we powerless.

Since we are finite beings, we must understand that the body is a machine with a limited supply of energy that needs to be cared for regularly in order for it to work well. How can we do this if we insist on ignoring the Manufacturer's instructions? The Bible tells us that we are designed for six days of activity and one day of repose. The day of sabbath is a gift that allows us to enjoy God and to let Him "recharge" us for the week ahead.

Why not plan your Sunday, or another day of the week so that there are a minimum of demands made on your physical and emotional energies. Can you, for instance, prepare your food the day before, or have foods you can simply heat or set out?

Join others in worship and/or go where you are able to contemplate the great works of God in creation. Be sure to include time to pray for those who in some way have contributed to your life (even those difficult people who have made you aware of the need for God in your life). Review your own spiritual history, just as biblical people have always done, including the special mechanism God used and is using to bring you to Himself.

As much as possible, do only those things which are truly recreational (*re-creational*), which refresh, replenish and strengthen you for the next six days of that week. Learn to listen to God's command, rather than your own or others' demands to do those things that sap your vitality.

Activities which foster this, I believe, are what God intends for the New Testament sabbath rest day. Rather than a way to earn favor, or a punishment for being human, sabbath rest is a gift of time to contemplate our bounty and our belovedness. Feast on art, music, nature, food, and fun. Rest emotionally and physically from work. Enjoy fellowship and relationships—particularly your relationship with God.

Recommended Activities

Unleash the Power of Scripture

Review the General Symptom Reducing Approaches listed in Lesson 3 of *Anxiety, Phobias & Panic*. Use a concordance (many Bibles have one in the back) to find a scripture that you think supports each.

Prepare or purchase some "Bible Promise Cards" to use daily, especially when feeling challenged or anxious. These are also helpful for memorizing Scripture.

Practice Sabbath Keeping

Discuss the role of the sabbath with someone who shares your life. How can you get the most out of this precious legacy? Establish a *"pray and play day,"* in which you make provision to:

- Repent the failures and sin of the previous week and accept the forgiveness that is yours in Christ.
- Gratefully contemplate God's creation, *including yourself*, and the provisions He has made for your restoration.
- Pray for those individuals, groups, and situations which compose your life.
- Plan recreation or play that refreshes you and helps you remember you are a *child* of God.

Renewing Your Mind

Supplement to Lesson 4

Even we Christians blame events or others for our emotions. "He makes me so mad!" "If she acted more Christian, I wouldn't feel this way!" "If God hadn't allowed this to happen to me, I wouldn't have to be so angry!"

This lesson looks at the way distorted thinking can contribute to anxiety and how perceptive spiritual insight can bring peace under the most trying circumstances.

Consider the story of Joseph, son of Israel and one of twelve brothers. The brothers resented their father's favoritism as well as Joseph's integrity and vision of his own exalted future. They allowed their jealousy to grow and fester until it led them to sell their youngest brother into slavery. Genesis 37, 39-50 tells how Joseph rose from slavery to power. In the house of Potiphar, who was the captain of Pharoah's body guard, Joseph suffered another injustice when Potiphar's wife falsely accused him of molesting her. This resulted in an eight year imprisonment for Joseph. He was released again and reached the height of privilege and power as prime minister of Egypt. Thirteen years after entering the country as a slave, his brothers came before him, begging for famine relief from this "Egyptian" leader, whom they did not recognize.

What were the emotions Joseph experienced after his cruel and unjust treatment from his brothers? Certainly one would expect rage and bitterness, yet without excusing or glossing over their behavior, we are surprised to find Joseph weeping with sadness and joy as he graciously welcomes them (Genesis 42:24, 43:30, 46:29).

It was Joseph's *interpretation of the events* that instructed his emotions and set him free from destructive hostility which would have increased his pain, and probably prevented his advancement as well. Instead, Joseph saw the experience of betrayal and injustice in a way that evoked the energy and motivation to live life fully and productively in a land and situation he did not choose.

Upon discovering that the Egyptian leader who held the power of life or death over them and their whole nation was actually their brother Joseph, the brothers were understandably terrified. But instead of finding him bitter towards them, Joseph said, "It was not you who sent me here, but God" (Genesis 45:7, 8).

Later, after years of gracious treatment from Joseph, the brothers' guilt and fear revived when their father died. Again, Joseph demonstrated how his interpretation of the events from a perspective of faith had freed him from the need for retribution and debilitating emotions which would accompany it. He assured them again, "You meant evil against me, but God meant it for good" (Genesis 50:20).

Each of us adopts habits of thinking by the time we are five or six years old that tend to stay with us for a life-time. Many of the assumptions and beliefs we develop at that time cause us to misinterpret events and assign inappropriate values to them. For example, our concept of God's will and ways at that age is incomplete at best. Perhaps this is why the experience of coming into a saving relationship with Jesus Christ is described as being "born again" or "anew" (John 3). It is a radical *transformation,* rather than adding a new bit of information about God. That beginning needs to take over our thinking—to change the way we see and interpret the world.

Paul says to those whose lives have been entered by Jesus Christ not to be "conformed to this world, but be transformed by *the renewing of your mind,* that you may prove (test along the way) what the will of God is, that which is good and acceptable and perfect" (Romans 12:3, italics added). In Christ we are able to confront the distorted thinking and irrational beliefs that produce destructive emotions. We can live in the same world while interpreting it differently.

The idea that this world is a place where everything is always fair and just is one such irrational belief. The Bible teaches that we live on a fallen planet awaiting the return of Christ when "the creation itself also will be set free from its slavery to corruption into the freedom of the glory of the children of God. For we know that the whole creation groans and suffers (until then)..." (Romans 8:21, 22). To expect that in the meantime people and events "should" or "must" behave in a fair way according to a universally accepted formula ignores the biblical description of the total catastrophe of the Fall. Everyone carries results of fallenness within.

On the other hand, to live with a sense of despair ignores what Scripture tells us about the sufficiency of God's redemption of creation through His Son. Though part of the fulfillment remains until He returns again at the end of the age, God has always made a provision for those who live according to the hope that is present in His promises. The Romans passage above goes on to say, "And we know that God causes all things to work together for good to those who love God, to those who are called according to His purpose" (Romans 8:26-28). So not only will the "new heaven and new earth" be a source of hope for us, but we are able to give new meaning to the events of our daily lives.

Isn't this what Joseph discovered? Life isn't always "fair." But even the seemingly tragic events and experiences of life can be redeemed by God and woven into the tapestry of one's life in a way that gives them purpose and meaning. This perspective enables us to challenge should/must and can't thinking and to substitute the terms "choose," "want," "like," and "prefer."

Recommended Activities

Unleash the Power of Scripture

Memorize all or part of the following verses:

This day I call heaven and earth as witnesses against you that I have set before you life and death, blessings and curses. Now choose life, so that you and your children may live and that you may love the Lord your God, listen to His voice, and hold fast to Him. For the Lord is your life, and He will give you many years in the land... (Deuteronomy 30:19, 20).

In what ways does this passage challenge the distorted thinking or irrational beliefs that one is a helpless victim, captive to emotions, circumstances or other people's treatment? Write your reflections about this below or in your journal, using the personal pronouns, I and me.

Take a Biblical Approach to "Shoulds" and "Musts"

Write an imaginary script about Joseph's life in Egypt in which you have Joseph using distorted thinking similar to the type you are studying. Choose either his self-talk while in prison (Genesis 39:20) or an imagined speech he might have made to his brothers (Genesis 45). Use as many "shoulds," "musts," and "can'ts" as you can cram in. Notice how Joseph's character seems to change when you have him talk like a victim.

Share your script with your prayer partner or someone else. Discuss how this form of distorted thinking might have changed Joseph's life. In prayer, reflect on how "should," "must", and "can't" thinking affects your life.

Gaining A Spiritual Perspective

Supplement to Lesson 5

Just as the Lord gives us a new perspective on life, His Spirit is at work within us changing the way we think. Jesus says, "If you abide in My word, you will know the truth, and the truth will make you free" (John 8:31, 32). The ten forms of distorted thinking can be challenged with many biblical verses or concepts. Distorted thinking can be another opportunity for the Spirit to work out our wholeness (holiness). While we can't control circumstances, we can remember that God is sovereign and rules over all life. God wants us to be active and responsible in bringing His rule over all creation. This includes our thought life.

Should/Must Thinking

From the first account of God's relationship with human beings, freedom of choice is emphasized (Genesis 2:16, 17). Our freedom is so important to Him that He even allows us to choose that which destroys us. But we need always remember that His desire is for us to select those things which give us abundant life. "I have set before you life and death, the blessing and the curse, choose life" (Deuteronomy 30:19).

The Lord wants us to include in our lives those things which enhance and set us free. The habit of thinking that we are compelled to do things, that we are helpless pawns, denies the basic quality of our being as ones created in God's own image.

All-or-Nothing Thinking

Sometimes people play the game of life, even the Christian life, as if it were an "elimination game," the kind of game where one mistake means you are out. Every error, each small failure, becomes the basis of major lament. But if the Lord tells us to forgive each other "up to seventy times seven" (Matthew 18:22), shouldn't we be as generous with ourselves? Some things don't even require forgiveness, just acceptance as part of our humanity. Everything is not a "salvation issue." In fact, the Bible teaches that only one thing is—our acceptance of Jesus Christ as our Lord and Savior, who Himself establishes our righteousness before God.

The next time you need to challenge all-or-nothing thinking, you might send up a silent prayer: "Thank you, Lord, that my eternal destiny does not depend on how well I do this particular task!" Or, "Lord, keep me from the temptation of bailing out of jobs, relationships, or goals because I perceive my mistakes or setbacks as catastrophic. Help me to hang in long enough to learn or contribute all that you would want in each situation."

Overgeneralization

Spiritually, overgeneralizations about how things "always" or "never" turn out tend to ignore that God is working to transform us. Even if we have performed in a certain way in the past, that is no reason to expect that we will *always* or *never* be different. David was not "always" an adulterer. Paul was not "always" thrown in jail. "Beloved, now we are children of God, and it has not appeared as yet what we shall be. We know that, when He appears, we shall be like Him, because we shall see Him just as He is" (1 John 3:2).

Labeling

The above verse can also serve to remind us that God does not label us "stupid," "incompetent," or other such denigrating names. Instead, we find ourselves called "beloved," "brother," "sister," "children of God," even "my perfect one" (Song of Songs 5:2). The Bible often tells of people receiving new names to show new life. At no time does God confuse our behavior with our worth. Instead, He makes provision for forgiveness of real sin for those who simply ask for it in Jesus name. And with this, we have a new name: *Forgiven.*

When you catch yourself using negative labels, try challenging them with something like, "Wait a minute. I'm not worthless. I simply made a mistake that anyone could make. I am so worthwhile that Christ died for me, even knowing that I would occasionally goof up."

Magnification/Minimization

Christine, the daughter of a missionary family in Mexico City, had already learned to challenge catastrophizing at age nine. "Mommy, it will be *terrible* if I can't go to the party," she said. Then, after a thoughtful pause she added, "Well, not *terrible* like the Ethiopian famine. But I sure want to go."

For a week, practice seeing the events in your life from the perspective and in the proportion that you think the Lord would see them. Not only will this help you to enjoy life more, but it will turn your wonderful sensitivity outward towards a hurting world.

On the other hand, sometimes we find ourselves paralyzed by minimizing the effect of our contribution. Remember God's response when Jeremiah said, "Alas, Lord God! I do not know how to speak because I am a youth."

"Do not say, 'I am a youth,' because everywhere I send you, you shall go, and all that I command you, you shall speak," (Jeremiah 1:6, 7) declares the Lord. Sometimes without even realizing it, we allow minimizing of our strengths to deprive ourselves and others of valuable participation.

The subject of spiritual gifts, especially as found in 1 Corinthians 12, Romans 12:3-8, and Ephesians 4:11-16, reminds us that each of us plays an essential role in God's plan.

Mind Reading

Putting the worst possible interpretation on the actions of others is the opposite of what the Lord wants us to do when He says through Paul, "Let us pursue the things which make for peace and the building up of one another" (Romans 14:19). Instead of "reading things into" another's mind, He urges us to "assume the faith" or the good will of those around us. And, "let us not judge (down) one another anymore, but rather determine this—not to put an obstacle or a stumbling block in a brother's (or sister's) way" (Romans 14:13).

Fortune Telling

Scripture is full of examples of men and women who were given the task of announcing future events. Prophets abound in both the Old and New Testaments. Yet, one must be careful not to take foreboding as the voice of God. They may be only part of a general anxiety or a habit of expecting the worst. Many claim a gift of "discernment" when what they are really manifesting are biases and distrust.

Accepting Questionable Sources as Authoritative

The Bible abounds in examples of this unhappy tendency. Remember Eve's counselor, the serpent, and his advice? "Did God really say, 'You must not eat from any tree in the garden?'...You will not surely die...For God knows that when you eat of it your eyes will be opened, and you will be like God, knowing good and evil" (Genesis 3:1-4).

Or consider Job's advisors who alternatively suggested that he "curse God and die" (his wife in Job 2:9) or that he confess the alleged sins which brought about all his misery. In reality, his suffering had nothing to do with his disobedience. These "comforters" couldn't see the larger picture partly because of their own envy of him and partly because of their ignorance.

Taking advice from someone is much like accepting him or her as your teacher. Jesus warns us to choose our teachers carefully: "A pupil is not above his teacher; but everyone, after he has been fully trained, will be like his teacher." In other words, taking advice tends to make you become like your advisor.

When you really need advice, ask in prayer to see the reliable people-resources the Lord provides for you. Pick only those whose example in that area is one you admire and regard as godly. When you already know what the Lord wants you to do, do it in spite of the warnings of those who might not have the whole picture or who might themselves be bound up by fear, jealousy, or ignorance.

Emotional Reasoning

We live in a culture obsessed with taking its emotional temperature and testing the emotional climate. Yet there are many things that we might choose to do even though they don't "feel good". Many unfamiliar things may cause momentary discomfort yet we can decide to do them because they are right or have a long-term benefit.

On the other hand, anxiety, depression, and anger often alert one to the need for rest and refreshment. A "burnt-out" Elijah was fed by an angel and made to sleep before he was able to regain his perspective and continue his work (1 Kings 19:4-7).

Emotions are part of the way that we are fearfully and wonderfully made (Psalm 139:14). They are *one* of the ways that we test whether we are on the right track in life. But feelings were never intended to be *sovereign* nor even the *primary* factor in making decisions. Emotions are simply a thermometer of whether some of our needs are being met. Emotions can be generated by spiritual needs as well as the mundane needs inherent in our "creatureliness." They can also be generated by distorted thinking and irrational beliefs. Because of this emotions always need to be balanced with reason and prayer. Christians must seek, value, and hold to the Truth as revealed in Scripture. Emotions alone may or may not indicate what the truth of a situation is.

Personalization

"I say to every one among you not to think more highly of him(her)self than (s)he ought to think; but to think so as to have sound judgement, as God has allotted to each..." (Romans 12:3). This passage refers to spiritual gifts, but it seems equally sound advice for those who personalize and take disproportionate responsibility for negative events.

While it *is* important to take responsibility for *real* offenses to God and others, false guilt is a weight that keeps us from relating to those around us in a sound way. Recognize that God alone is all-powerful. The freedom of choice that He gives us is also a gift to everyone else with whom we come into contact. This frees us from thinking we control events or the happiness of others.

Notice the conditional tone of this verse: "*If possible, so far as it depends on you*, be at peace with all..." (Romans 12:18, italics added). When you are inclined to feel guilty about another's mood or the outcome of some event, check your part in it with the above two quotes. One way to do this is to ask yourself the following three questions:

- "Am I thinking more highly of myself than I ought regarding my influence in this?"
- "So far as it depends on me, am I contributing peace to this?"
- "If I truly find myself at fault, am I able to confess it to the Lord (and others when appropriate) and move on?"

Recommended Activities

Assuming The Faith

During this week, challenge yourself by "assuming the faith" of those around you and the power of the Lord to work in the new situation to which He has called you. List on paper or in prayer those times when God has equipped you to learn a new skill or to succeed in a new task. This will remind you that the negative predictions you sometimes make aren't always reflective of the past. Nor are they binding on how the Lord may be working in you or your life in the future.

Study Spiritual Gifts

Read 1 Corinthians 12, Romans 12:3-8, and Ephesians 4:11-16 on spiritual gifts. Write here or in your journal the verses that argue against exaggerating or minimizing one's contribution in the family of faith.

Adequate Servanthood

Supplement to Lesson 6

"If something is worth doing for the Lord, it should be done excellently!" This truism (something which appears on the surface to be true but on closer examination may not be true) can be a trap for Christians who exhaust or paralyze themselves with perfectionistic demands. Instead of being liberated and energized by their faith, they make God one more harsh taskmaster. In a sense, this illustrates the common tendency to "baptize our pathologies" when we become Christians. Instead of allowing Christ to strip us of those things that limit us, we attempt to camouflage them as Christian virtues.

Thinking that one must do everything excellently is a form of perfectionistic distortion. This implies that doing anything less than perfectly is worse than not doing it at all. It also takes the joy out of participating as well as keeping us from enjoying others' contributions. Instead, we are always comparing our efforts with others' and wondering what might have been done to make it better.

A frequently cited verse used to reinforce this notion is from Matthew 5:48, where Jesus says: "Therefore, you are to be perfect as your heavenly Father is perfect." This troubling verse needs careful examination.

The word "perfect" could better be translated "mature" or "complete." Earl Palmer, author and pastor, compares the use of the word in this passage to that of the ideal Greek statue; it was perfect in that it was cut of one piece of stone, without added-on limbs. This is the sense in which we are to be perfect in the love (for love is Jesus' subject here) that we manifest as Christians. Our love is to be mature and complete. It is a love of others that not only refrains from murder, adultery, and retaliation, but one that perseveres in relationships and seeks reconciliation (Matthew 5:17-48). It is not "tacked on" for effect, but permeates both our behavior and our attitudes. Such a love is perfect in that it is complete and mature.

We need to remember also that *God* is the Sculptor and we are the statues. No statue sculpts itself. We are in a life-time process of being perfected in love. We yield ourselves to that process, while God, through His indwelling Spirit, takes the responsibility for our perfection in love. This is not something that happens overnight, nor is it a demand by God that we do everything excellently or not at all.

> Beloved, now we are children of God, and it has not appeared as yet what we shall be. We know that when He appears, we shall be like Him, because we shall see Him just as He is. And everyone who has this hope fixed on Him purifies himself, just as He is pure (1 John 3:2, 3).

This assures us that our purity (or perfection) resides in our hope fixed on Jesus, not in our performance. Therefore it is futile to whip ourselves with perfectionistic demands. Instead, may I recommend "The High Call of Mediocrity" as a more realistic ambition for a believer-in-process? Or we might prefer more biblical language and aspire to "The High Call of *Adequate Servanthood*".

> And such confidence we have through Christ toward God. Not that we are adequate in ourselves to consider anything as coming from ourselves, but our adequacy is from God, who also made us adequate servants of a new covenant, not of the letter (perfectionism), but of the Spirit; for the letter (perfectionism) kills, but the Spirit gives life (2 Corinthians 3:4-6).

Paul also says that we are to be students of Scripture in order "that the man (and woman) of God may be *adequate*, equipped for every good work" (2 Timothy 4:17). Not *perfect*—just *adequate* and *equipped*.

Self-talk that is helpful to confront this tendency towards perfectionism might go something like this:

> "The fall of woman and man was the result of not accepting the limits placed on them by God and by their desire for equal status with God. I am deceived when I

think I must do everything perfectly. God only wants me to try as best I am able and to obey His will as I understand it."

Another challenge to perfectionism comes in a discussion of spiritual gifts and ministries in 1 Corinthians 12:6: "And there are varieties of effects, but the same God who works all things in all."

This affirms that God Himself takes responsibility for the outcome or the empowerment of any action done to bring Him glory. In other words, the same effort done on behalf of the Kingdom, can have different "voltage" in various cases. This indicates that our job is to be obedient, as He gives us to understand what that means in any given situation or task. He decides the outcome. No need to compare or regret. Just give it your best effort!

Neither is it given to finite, limited beings such as we humans to be in total control of all situations. Only God has this kind of power. And though He does not always permit us to know the outcome or even the reasons for the things He calls us to do, He still wants us to act in response to His call in our lives. There are no 100% guarantees that events will go as *we* want them to go. Instead, just as we must simply be adequate servants, we must in faith give over control to the Lord, waiting for Him to reveal what part we have played in His over-all design.

Recommended Activities

Learn to be an Adequate Servant

Review the scriptures in this lesson (Matthew 5:17-48; 1 John 3:2, 3; 2 Corinthians 3:4-6). Record in your journal or below your reflections on "The High Call of Mediocrity" or "Adequate Servanthood". Comment on the freedom you find in this attitude.

Do something at which you are only adequate. Before doing the activity, list the benefits of doing it even if you "lose" or do not excel. For example, if you decide to play nine holes of golf with a friend who is better than you, you can enjoy being out of doors, watching birds, the sky, and the variety of plants; enjoy talking and exercising; or even enjoy your friend enjoying beating you!

Supplement to Lesson 7

Cast Your Burdens On The Lord

One of the most unpleasant effects of anxiety-related problems is the tendency at times to worry about almost everything. The Lord knows us well, we see from His words in the Sermon on the Mount discourse:

> Do not be anxious then, saying "What shall we eat?" or "What shall we drink?" or "With what shall we clothe ourselves?"...for your heavenly Father knows that you need all these things (Matthew 6:31, 32).

These questions are part of an over-arching "What if" attitude many experience as they approach activities. Somehow every unlikely negative possibility seems to present itself. Even common endeavors can seem full of risks and dangers.

In the last lesson we challenged the need to be in control constantly and have a 100% guarantee of a certain outcome before we set out on a task. We also considered the freedom that is ours when we grasp that the Lord is in control, not we. The Gospel of Mark shows Jesus as the Shepherd Who is continually going before and asking His disciples to follow, to be *with* Him.

Each year at Christmas we are reminded that He is "Emmanuel—which means, 'God with us' " (Matthew 1:23). He came to be with us in both our joy and difficulties. And nothing can break this bond for which He takes responsibility:

> Who shall separate us from the love of Christ? Shall tribulation, or distress, or persecution, or famine, or nakedness, or peril, or work?...For I am convinced that neither death, nor life, nor angels, nor principalities, nor things present, nor things to come, nor powers, nor height, nor depth, nor any other created thing, shall be able to separate us from the love of God, which is in Christ Jesus the Lord (Romans 8:35-39).

In an ultimate sense, we *do* have a 100% guarantee. We *do* know the final outcome. And although nobody knows for certain how each event or situation in life will turn out, we have the promise that whatever life throws at us, Jesus Christ will be with us. If we ask for His presence as Lord and Savior, He will be there. "Lo, I am always with you, even unto the end of the age," He promised His followers (Matthew 28:10).

Taking Responsibility for Your Life

Since God is in control, does the Bible suggest that we are merely pawns or robots? Not at all. From Genesis on, the Bible teaches that though God loves us and created us for a relationship with Him, He wants us to freely choose life with Him. We are responsible for maintaining our relationships and for owning up to those things we do that damage these relationships.

The main difference between the Apostle Peter and Judas was *not* that one was unfailingly faithful to the Lord and the other betrayed Him. Instead, it was that Judas saw himself as a victim in life and habitually blamed others for his disappointments and behavior. In a series of descending steps, Judas blamed the Romans for ruining his life by subjugating his country, blamed Jesus for not fulfilling Judas' idea of the revolutionary role of the Messiah, then blamed the Jewish leaders when his attempt to force Jesus' hand failed. Finally, his consuming blame and lack of forgiveness of himself resulted in his giving up on life and on the Lord.

Peter also betrayed the Lord on that last day. But he faced his sin and responsibility in a way that was both productive and restorative. Peter stayed with other believers and ran to the tomb seeking the risen Lord, whom he had so recently denied not once but three times. Thus, the Lord required him to confess his devotion the same number of times that Peter had denied Him. Then instead of dwelling on Peter's failure, Christ told him to get on with his work: "Feed My sheep" (John 21:15-17).

As believers, we are commanded to face the responsibility of our own sin, neither blaming someone else for it, nor condemning ourselves whom Christ has saved by His blood. The sacrifice has been made on Calvary. What is required of us is facing our sin and turning from it to the One Who saves. God has promised forgiveness and restoration in the Lord Jesus. But He doesn't forgive *excuses.* He forgives sin. Repentance is to the spiritual life what responsibility is to the mature life. In both cases we are to face our errors realistically; but we are not given the power to condemn—even ourselves.

We are invited to face any challenge knowing that Jesus is with us. Coming to know this will help you replace "What if.." with "*So what* if...?" Because "we know that God causes all things to work together for good to those who love God, to those who are called according to His purpose" (Romans 8:28), we have ample reason to live as positive realists.

That's Not Fair

One of the distortions of attitude carried over from childhood is the final, frustrated protest of the mightily offended: "That's not fair!" Whoever said life on this planet is *fair*? We've already seen how the Fall disrupted God's original intention for humankind. Yet often when we meet with difficulties, disappointments, or injustices, we take up the primal howl, "No fair!"

If ever one had the right to cry foul, it was our Lord. Though Jesus was "holy, innocent, undefiled, separated from sinners, and exalted above the heavens" (Hebrew 7:26), "God made Him who knew no sin to be sin on our behalf, that we might become the righteousness of God in Him" (2 Corinthians 5:21). He "was delivered up (to execution) because of *our* transgressions" Romans 4:25). "He was oppressed and He was afflicted, yet He did not open His mouth, like a lamb that is led to the slaughter, and like a sheep that is silent before its shearers, so He did not open his mouth" (Isaiah 5:3-7).

Since our Lord was not treated with fairness, why do we expect that we will be treated fairly at all times? Life is not fair. Yet we live in the certain knowledge that *God is not only fair* but He is merciful and will somehow work together all the elements of our lives to cause us to become the persons He wants us to be. "If God be for me, who can be against me?" There is no "what if..." powerful enough to thwart God as He works a transformation in the life of one of His own.

Recommended Activities

Unleashing the Power of Scripture and Prayer

Read Matthew 6:25-34 several times this week and consider how the Lord acknowledges our tendency towards negative anticipation. Write Him a "prayer letter," thanking Him for the way He anticipates your fears and speaks to them in His Word.

Memorize the bottom line of the scripture passage you looked at: "Therefore do not worry about tomorrow, for tomorrow will worry about itself. Each day has enough trouble of its own," or, the King James Version, "Let the evil of the day be sufficient therein."

It is reassuring to know that "your heavenly Father knows that you need (all these things)." Yet, you may find that when it comes to anxiety about specific upcoming experiences, simply reminding yourself about God's care and provision for you isn't enough to break this worry habit. When this is the case, *prayerfully* go through the "Four-Step Approach" suggested in Lesson 7 of *Anxiety, Phobias & Panic*. Then pray that the Lord will reveal a plan of action for you, and that He will walk through the event with you.

Supplement to Lesson 8

As One Approved

David was tested by the most difficult of tasks. He was put under the authority of and in frequent contact with King Saul. While Saul depended on David, he was also consumed by irrational jealousy and hatred of him. The story of Saul and David is found in 1 Samuel 16-31. The book, *A Tale of Three Kings: A Study in Brokenness*, by Gene Edwards, dramatically demonstrates the three statements to memorize in Lesson 8 of *Anxiety, Phobias & Panic* on page 114. Let's look at these three statements in light of the story of David.

People are frequently unable to express warmth and acceptance for reasons having nothing to do with myself.

The Bible presents David as a faithful servant to King Saul. At first, the king loved David and made him his personal armor bearer. However, Saul allowed jealousy of his young protege to dominate and eventually destroy the relationship.

People often react negatively towards things I do for irrational reasons.

As David played his harp to soothe his king, Saul hurled a spear at him. What a futile exercise it would have been for David to indulge in the kinds of self-talk characteristic of an excessive need for approval listed on pages 116-118 of *Anxiety, Phobias & Panic*. Read these examples over as if David were saying them. This should provide you more than a chuckle, as you put David's and Saul's names into it!

There will always be a small percentage of people I deal with who just won't like me no matter what I do, usually for irrational reasons.

We are told that while Saul was hostile towards David: "all Israel and Judah loved David, and he went out and came in before them" (1 Samuel 18:16). Though he was in the confusing predicament of being part of the inner circle of a king who sometimes loved him and increasingly hated him, David kept his perspective. He did this, I believe, partly by continually renewing his confidence in God with the songs he composed. Also, he went in and out among the vast majority of people who thought highly of him. This reminded him that as devastating as it must have was to be rejected by the great King Saul, it was not due to anything he had or hadn't done.

The faithful, like David, are often easy prey to the irrational demands of others. And some mistakenly equate people-pleasing philosophies with Christian love. But our very status as servants of Christ calls us to another allegiance. As Paul puts it, "Am I now trying to win the approval of men, or of God?...If I were still trying to please men, I would not be a servant of Christ" (Galatians 1:10).

As those who belong to Christ, we are called to *koinonia*, that close fellowship of interdependence that the Bible likens to being part of one body. Yet even in our relationship with other believers, we will not always be accepted and understood. Sometimes, for reasons that have nothing to do with us, we will meet with rejection and even hostility.

This is how little the Lord trusted popularity: "Woe to you when all men speak well of you, for in the same way their fathers used to treat the false prophets" (Luke 6:26). However, this is not a recommendation for bitterness or a cynical attitude towards others. "But I say to you who hear, love your enemies, do good to those who hate you" (Luke 6:27).

Faith-Inspired Challenges

Following are the self-talk examples showing an excessive need for approval listed on page 116 of *Anxiety, Phobias & Panic* along with faith-inspired challenges you can use to counter them.

1. "If someone important to me expects me to do something, I should do it."

    "After I've prayed about it and I truly believe God wants me to, I will try to respond to the needs around me."

Supplement to Lesson 8: As One Approved

2. "I'm not doing enough; I should do more."

    "While I may feel I should do more, I know that God wants me to have a rhythm of work, worship, and play in my life."

3. "I should do what people expect me to do."

    "I delight to do thy will O my God" (Psalm 40:8).

4. "I shouldn't be irritable or unpleasant."

    "When I'm angry or irritable, I need to see if God wants me to rest or to take action."

5. "I shouldn't make others angry at me."

    "While I would like to have others' approval and appreciation, the approval of others isn't necessary for me to do what I've prayerfully decided to do."

6. "I should keep people I love happy."

    "Lord, (person's name) is so unhappy. I have no power to change that, but I know you can work in his/her life and I give him/her over to you."

7. "It's my fault he/she is upset."

    "Because I've given (person's name) to your care, Father, I will not take responsibility for his/her moods."

8. "Rejection is the worst thing that can happen."

    "Rejection hurts but in it I have fellowship with Jesus and David who also experienced it."

9. "I can't be happy if others don't like me."

    "My happiness is based on God's unfailing love. He will never leave me nor forsake me."

10. "I can't stand being alone."

    "I can never be alone when I seek the presence of the Lord."

11. "I'm nothing unless I'm loved."

    "Jesus loves me, and by His cross proves my value to Him."

12. "It's terrible when I'm not noticed."

"Lord, I know that as I humble myself under your mighty hand, you will exalt me in due time" (1 Peter 5:8a).

13. "I need to be understood."

"The One who understands me best loves me most."

14. "Others should show appreciation for what I do."

"Though I would like others to appreciate me, what is important is that I be approved in Christ and that He shine through me."

Think of the Lord Jesus Christ. Though He was God, He was also fully human and like us in all ways except that He was without sin. He was not immune to the pain that came with rejection and persecution. In fact, since He was aware that rejection of Him had eternal consequences, it seems fair to assume that His pain was much greater than ours when we are rejected.

How comforting to know that He understands how we feel when we fail to gain the understanding and acceptance of those around us! Add to this the awareness that He loves you and personally experiences *your* pain as well, and there is much comfort. If you have entrusted your life and eternal destiny to His care, know that you already have His full approval. Therefore, "present yourself to God as one approved, a workman (or woman) who does not need to be ashamed" (2 Timothy 2:15).

Supplement to Lesson 8: As One Approved

Recommended Activities

Planning a Productive Time of Solitude

Throughout the ages Christians have kept a time of solitude, incorporating several disciplines of the faith. Lesson 8 of *Anxiety, Phobias & Panic* suggests keeping a journal. This is one of the ways to maintain a vital spiritual life of reflection and prayer. Perhaps this is already your practice. One such pattern for a productive period of solitude follows. It is helpful to have a regular time several days a week.

- Choose a place that is peaceful and free of distractions. A few minutes of relaxed breathing while meditating on nature, a picture of the Lord or with closed eyes is a good way to become aware of God's presence.
- Meditate on God's word and be like a tree planted by streams of water, says the introduction to the Psalms (Psalms 1:2, 3). Read and reflect on a short passage of Scripture, perhaps going sequentially through the Psalms. Note in your journal the passages which particularly speak to you; or rewrite the verses, putting your name and circumstances into them.
- List your specific petitions (You may want to reverse this pattern and read the Bible before making your list. It is amazing to see how the Lord answers with a relevant verse the concerns you have just raised).
- In prayer, relinquish your burdens to God. Commit each person or issue to the Lord. Wait quietly to receive God's blessing for you.
- As you write in your journal, reflect on those persons whose approval you feel you need. Ask the Lord to show you if this need is excessive or is keeping you from enjoying the acceptance that is yours as one set free by Jesus.

Use Psalm 55 as an Antidote to Fears of Rejection.

As you work through this lesson, use Psalm 55 as an antidote to fears of rejection. David knew rejection from others as well as Saul. His own son, Absalom, led a palace revolt against King David (2 Samuel 14). Psalm 55 tells of the pain David suffered as a result of betrayal by an intimate, believing friend. Copy into your journal those phrases that seem to fit your situation or fears, as well as those words which bring promise of comfort.

Supplement to Lesson 9

Connecting With the Body of Christ

Worship is the central and centering experience for believers. It is here that we are taught and empowered to live the Christian life.

Many peoples will come and say, "Come, let us go up to the mountain of the Lord, to the house of the God of Jacob; that He may teach us concerning His ways, and that we may walk in His paths" (Isaiah 2:3).

Sometimes problems with anxiety keeps a person away from vital participation in church activities. Listen to the anguish of a person who felt separated from God and unable to worship.

These things I remember, and I pour out my soul within me. For I used to go along with the throng and lead them in procession to the house of God, with the voice of joy and thanksgiving, a multitude keeping festival (Psalm 42:4).

Are avoidance patterns interfering with your ability to enjoy worship and fellowship with others? Or, do they keep you from participating in ministries you would like to join?

As in the other areas of life, you begin by identifying specifically the problem behaviors associated with your religious life. Look at the following list and check any situations that are difficult for you. Add any others you think of that are not on the list.

Mingling with a crowd
Shaking hands
Talking with strangers
Taking part in small groups
Singing or reading aloud
Taking refreshments
Sitting in the middle of a pew
Praying aloud in a group

Having identified those situations that are difficult for you, select one you wish to overcome. Break this goal into a series of steps as described in Lesson 9 of *Anxiety, Phobias & Panic*. For instance, if your goal is sitting in the middle of a pew at a worship service, your steps might be:

1. Arrive early. Sit next to the aisle. If someone asks you to move in, smile and say, "I need to be on the aisle. I might have to leave."
2. Go with a support person. Have your support person sit next to the aisle.
3. Bring two friends who will sit in positions one and two with you in three.
4. Sit with a support person a third of the way into an aisle. If the seats around you fill up and you become anxious, practice your relaxation techniques, making sure you are breathing with your diaphragm. Distract yourself by reading the bulletin, Bible, or hymnal. Two other forms of distraction you can use are memorizing verses or taking time to notice the symbols and details of the sanctuary and considering how each contributes to an atmosphere of worship. Take notes during the sermon—the preacher will be impressed and flattered!.

When using gradual *in vivo* exposure, remember always to begin by exposing yourself to those parts of worship or other activities which are less stressful. For instance, by coming late and leaving during the last hymn, you will be able to avoid much of the usual contact, and the crowded aisles that may cause discomfort. You may want to try sitting in different areas of the sanctuary to see which you find the best for you. Some churches have balconies, adjacent rooms, prayer or "crying rooms" which are less crowded and will offer you more privacy. Your church may also offer alternative services which are less crowded.

Keep a list of your coping skills in your Bible, pocket, or purse. The sanctuary is an ideal place to close your eyes, take time to breathe, and concentrate on these skills. Even in the most friendly and informal congregations, people seldom intrude if someone seems to be meditating, praying, or reading Scripture. There are certainly lots of ways to distract yourself from physical symptoms as you study the diversity of people in the choir and pews, the architectural features, or read from the prayer book or hymnal.

Some of the distortions that add to anxieties associated with church attendance may come in the sermon, hymns, appeals, or other messages you receive there. If you are a person with perfectionistic demands on yourself, part of your avoidance may be due to the feeling that you must respond to every call. Remember that many people are there with you. What one person needs to hear may not apply to the next one in the row. Instead, always prepare for worship with a time of prayer that the Lord will give you "ears to hear and eyes to see" that which He has meant *for you*. Don't let the supersensitivity that often goes with these problems deprive you of being with God and His people. Everyone, without exception, comes with needs. Your needs are in no way more or less shameful or insolvable than the person next to you in the pew.

Consider speaking to your pastor about your problems and the program you are using to overcome them. Your pastor will either understand immediately, or you may have the privilege of being God's instrument to educate that pastor. This will add to the pastor's skills and utility in ministry. Wouldn't it be wonderful to know that even as you go through your dark valley, the Lord is using your problems to enrich the community of faith?

Recommended Activities

Rejoin the Body of Christ

If your anxiety-related problem has kept you from enjoying the community of faith, do the following this week.

- Set as your goal, regular participation in a church of your choice.
- Write about this in your journal before the Lord.
- Read a Psalm, selecting a line which speaks to your fears.
- Make a step-by-step plan for confronting this fear and freeing yourself from its control over your worship life.
- Pray, committing every detail of your plan to the Lord. When He told you to take His easy yoke upon you, He had already placed Himself in the other half. It is an easy yoke because He pulls with you (Matthew 11:29, 30).

Supplement to Lesson 10

Transformation

Change is not only *recommended* in the Bible, it is *commanded*. This change is not some minor modification meant to spruce us up a bit on the outside. It is so complete and integral to one's being, it is called *transformation*. "Be transformed by the renewing of your mind," says Romans 12:2. This word is from the same root as *metamorphosis*, that process whereby a caterpillar becomes a butterfly. Certainly it is not a magic "zapping" that changes one instantaneously. It is a series of *becomings*, in which you yield yourself to a step-by-step, layer-by-layer transformation.

Paul insists that in this process we focus on the person of Jesus. "We all, with unveiled face beholding as in a mirror the glory of the Lord, are being transformed into the same image from glory to glory" (2 Corinthians 3:18). Our "unveiled faces" represent that realistic assessment of who we are and in what ways we tend to resist the changes the Lord has in mind for us. That is why it is so essential to constantly look into the "mirror of Christ's glory." That is where we see the reflection of the character and freedom He has in mind for us.

Later, in 5:17, Paul says, "If anyone is in Christ, he is a new creature; the old things passed away; behold new things have come." This reminds us that change is the expected, the unavoidable condition of being a Christian.

People who read the Bible thoughtfully know that even though the real change is brought about by God, He honors our freedom and wants our permission and participation. Of the man by the pool of Bethesda who had been afflicted for thirty-eight years, Jesus asked, "Do you want to get well?" (John 5:6).

In the same way, though *He* ultimately works our transformation, He wants us to "walk out our salvation (transformation)"—to go through the steps He sets before us.

So then, my beloved, just as you have always obeyed,...work out your salvation with fear and trembling; for it is God who is at work in you, both to will and to work for His good pleasure (Philippians 2:12-13).

This process is not without pain and difficulty. All change is filled with times of confusion and struggle. Paul's life was certainly filled with upheaval, but he regarded his suffering as a tool for spiritual change:

We rejoice in our suffering, knowing that suffering produces endurance; and endurance produces character; and character produces hope; and that hope does not disappoint us, because God's love is poured into our hearts through the Holy Spirit, which is given to us (Romans 5:3-5).

Is transformation easy and painless? No, but think what the caterpillar would have missed if it hadn't entered the cocoon! In *The Voyage of the Dawntreader* by C.S. Lewis there is a marvelous allegory of how pain is often a necessary element of change. Eustace, one of the children on an adventure, has changed into a dragon. As the boy-dragon lies weeping amid a treasure, Aslan, a great lion who is the Christ-figure of the Narnia tales, arrives to change Eustace back into a boy. Layer by layer Aslan's sharp claws tear at the dragon skin until they reach the tender, pink boy flesh beneath. Stinging, but free of his "dragonness," Eustace enters the cool, clear pool where his transformation is completed.

Recommended Activities

Unleash the Power of Prayer

During this week, take time to prayerfully review your life. List the things God has changed in your life. Perhaps you specifically prayed about these, perhaps not. Thank the Lord for changing those circumstances or habits.

After you have completed your review, list before the Lord your concerns about those habits or anxieties which still are an undesirable part of your life. Richard Foster describes an excellent way of doing this in *Celebration of Discipline* that he calls a "hands down, hands up" exercise in prayer. As you name your concerns, have your hands down on your lap. Then, as you give your burden over to Jesus, turn your hands up. Keep this receptive hands up position as you use relaxed diaphragmatic breathing. Wait in silence as God gives you His peace, a practical idea for dealing with your situation, or insight into the process He is using to change you. After a while, reflect on what you have heard or learned, writing below or in your prayer journal.

Removing the Dragon Skin

Just like the dragon skin that entrapped Eustace, we have things that God wants to strip away from us. In your journal, reflect on those evidences of "dragonness" that need Christ's transforming touch. Also, list the layers (these may be attitudes, habits, behaviors, or even people) that the Lord has already removed in order to help you emerge as the person He intends you to be.

Celebrating God's Work In You

Supplement to Lesson 11

God included you in the created world which He called "good." As if this foundation were not enough, He added His Son to this statement about our worth. The cornerstone of our self-esteem is none other than Jesus Christ. Bought with such a price, our worth is established beyond question. God loves us enough to die for us, to live in and through us by His Holy Spirit. Jesus intercedes for us before the throne of grace. He will return for us at the end of the age and take us to live forever in God's presence.

> Here I am! I stand at the door and knock; if anyone hears My voice and opens the door, I will come in and eat with him, and he with Me. To him who overcomes, I will give the right to sit with Me on My throne, just as I overcame and sat down with My Father on His throne (Revelation 3:20, 21).

This should suffice to take away all of our doubts about our value. But we live on a planet that is distorted by the Fall. The image of God that is within every human who ever lived, is veiled with flesh which is subject to distortion. For us, the "overcoming" referred to in the verses above is that of overcoming the rebellious tendency to shut Christ out, to deny the declaration He has made about our worth and the power we have to live righteous lives.

Just as transformation is not an option for the believer, neither is accepting our own value. To continue to see ourselves as worthless and to regard change as hopeless, is to deny the gospel—the good news that in Jesus the righteousness of God has broken into our very lives (see Romans 1:16, 17). If having the power of God available in our lives because of Christ counts for nothing, then surely He died in vain. And we know that is not true! Instead, let's live expectantly.

Perhaps you are reluctant to practice the "mirror talk" as suggested in Lesson 11 of *Anxiety, Phobias & Panic* because it seems like bragging. If so, why not turn it into an opportunity for thanking God for investing His image in you or thanking Him for the process of change that you see happening as you go through this program? Try putting it something like this:

"Thank You, Lord, for the ability to sing so well. And I like me."
"Thank You, Lord, that with Your help I am becoming assertive as I understand my value to You. And I like myself more as I see Your love for me."

You can also use your prayer journal to record those things about yourself that God wants you to embrace and enjoy as gifts from Him. It is amazing to think that God is able to use or transform everything about us to His glory. Did you ever stop to think that through you, with your flaws, weaknesses, and even past sins, God can reach people who struggle in the same ways? That is what is meant by the words in Joel 2:25, "I will restore to you the years that the locust has eaten." Even those years that seem wasted become valuable as you offer them up to Him.

Compliments In Scripture

When you review some of the compliments given by the Lord and others in Scripture, notice that they are specific, often obvious and simple, rather than extravagant or "gushy." Look at Paul's compliments to both men and women found in Philippians 2:19-30, and in Romans 16:1-12. The Lord Jesus also expressed His appreciation of many individuals. For instance, see what He says to Nathaniel in John 1:47 and to Mary in Luke 10:42. Make a list of these and other biblical compliments. Try to think of those you know today about whom these things could be said. Then plan how to pass on such compliments person-to-person or in a note.

Read in its entirety Solomon's Song of Songs. If you are married, this makes for a wonderful dialogue between you and your spouse as you read it aloud together. Many Bibles give headings for the husband's, wife's, and other parts. While on one level, this book is a celebration of married love, at its deepest, it is a description of God's love for His beloved church and each believer. Even if you are single, Song of Songs and its compliments are for you.

Commitments

Sometimes we need to challenge the notion that "good Christians" say yes to every request. Though we are called to servanthood, we are servants of the Lord and not slaves to every demand around us. As His servants, we need to be obedient to *His* agenda for us. If He is in the process of healing us or if He has enrolled us in a new course in the school of life, that is where we need to be.

Be slow to commit yourself to new projects. Take time to pray about each. Discuss them with your spiritual friend if you find you need counsel or support. When you feel you should decline, resist giving long explanations. Rather, when appropriate, say, "I have prayed about it and feel I must say no." If you think the person would not understand this answer, simply say, "I have decided I must say no to your request." If they ask why or plead with you to reconsider, just be a "broken record" and repeat yourself: "No, I've given this a lot of prayer (or thought), and I have decided I won't be doing it."

Comparing Yourself With Others

The familiar story known as "The Parable of the Prodigal Son" (Luke 15:11-32) is helpful not only to remind ourselves of God's special love for each of His children, but also to warn us of the tendency to compare ourselves and our treatment with others.

Paul reminds us that everyone has a part to play in God's scheme of things: "I planted, Apollos watered, but God was causing the growth" (1 Corinthians 3:6). He also shows his healthy sense of self when he refuses to let others critique his life:

> But to me it is a very small thing that I should be examined by you, or by any human court; in fact, I do not even examine myself. I am conscious of nothing against myself, yet I am not by this acquitted; but the one who examines me is the Lord. Therefore, do not go on passing judgment before the time, but wait until the Lord comes who will both bring to light the things hidden...and disclose the motives of hearts; and then each one's *praise* will come to him from God (1 Corinthians 4:3-5).

I have added the emphasis on the word *praise* to show that when God comes to understand those who are His through Christ, it is not to judge but to reward us. He knows our struggle and the motives of our hearts. He does not compare us to others who perhaps have more "native ability" or less to contend with in life.

Recommended Activities

Celebrate His Work In You

Each day that you work on this lesson, choose one of the passages of scripture on which to meditate. Rewrite it, personalizing it by adding your name and the details of your situation. Using your journal, list those things about yourself that you believe come from God, heading it "Thank you, Lord, for..." Use this list when you practice your "mirror talk."

Work With Compliments

Review the compliments in Scripture listed in this lesson. Then write a note, make a call, or speak face-to-face with someone, affirming or complimenting them. Be specific, simple, and descriptive of an action or quality you appreciate in him or her.

Review Your Commitments

Review your commitments. Are there any that are worrisome to you? If so, pray about them. If you feel that they should be set aside, call those involved and take care of it.

Supplement to Lesson 12

Anger—God's Confusing Gift

Anger is a difficult emotion for many Christians. Some equate it with sin and conclude, "I should never feel or express anger." Others allow for anger but only for the important things that they see as "legitimate concerns" of God and the godly such as the inhumanity people show towards each other, religious apostasy, and flagrant sinfulness.

Some of the angriest people around, both in and out of the church, are those who deny that they ever feel anger and those who haven't learned to express anger appropriately. Unable to interpret or apply anger properly, some pass it off as holy zeal. They may become the watch dogs of orthodoxy or militants against anything they see as threatening the purity of the church. Instead of presenting a gospel of grace and love they substitute a message of criticism.

Thoughtful Christians, however, can see that anger along with the other emotions is part of the way that we are fearfully and wonderfully made in the image of God. Scanning the Old and New Testaments, we find that God expresses the full range of emotions: joy, sorrow, anger, and love. This helps us understand that all emotions are part of the good created order. This is true of anger as well as the other emotions. As with the other parts of our being, such as our hands, the question is not, "How do I get rid of it?" but "How do I use my emotions as I become the person God wants me to be?"

Lesson 12 in *Anxiety, Phobias & Panic* shows how anger is useful for mustering our energy in the face of threat and motivating us to change in our lives. In the Bible we see various forms and degrees of anger, ranging from irritation to rage, expressed by the Lord. We notice that His anger is always in response to threats posed to the purposes for which Christ came. These threats are quickly identified. God's anger is appropriately focused and proportionately expressed.

When the woman described in John 8:2-11 was taken in adultery by men who were ignoring their own sin while exposing her's, Jesus quietly waited, writing in the dirt before He responded. Perhaps He was using His anger towards their self-righteousness and also towards her sin as He composed the perfect answer. This answer not only acknowledged the seriousness of the sin but their hypocrisy: "If anyone of you is without sin, let him be the first to throw a stone at her" (John 8:7).

On several occasions, Jesus expressed irritation at things said or done by those He loved and with whom He chose to share life. Even to Peter, one of His inner circle, He said angrily, "Get behind me, Satan; for you are not setting your mind on God's interests, but man's" (Mark 8:33).

Notice, it was the "set of Peter's mind" and not Peter himself that was the focus of His anger. Calling Peter "Satan" was Jesus' way of personifying that which threatened the very purpose of Christ's coming to Earth. He came to die on the cross in order to pay the price for our sins. Had He failed to do so, Jesus would have been just another good example, and Satan would have won.

At both the beginning and the end of His public ministry, Jesus is shown racing through the courts of the temple, whip in hand, overturning the tables of those who were defiling His Father's house. This is a vivid picture of rage—appropriate rage—at the corrupting of worship and their hindering access to God.

The Bible does *not* equate anger with sin. It does, however, warn that anger can be an opportunity for sin. Paul says, "In your anger, do not sin. Do not let the sun go down while you are still angry, and do not give the devil a foothold" (Ephesians 4:26).

The Psalmist gives us a little bit longer (until morning) saying, "In your anger do not sin; when you are on your beds, search your hearts and be still" (Psalm 4:4). It is clear, we see, that anger is something to be acknowledged and dealt with. If your anger has caused you to hurt someone unnecessarily or violate a person's rights, you need to make that right as soon as possible. Then you will be able to rest, knowing you have done what God asks of you.

Suggestions for Christians Who Think Anger Is "Sinful"

Like everything else in your life, your ability to feel and express anger serves a purpose or God would not have included it in your make-up. When you allow someone to intimidate you, you are hurting the person who is intimidating you as well as your own self-esteem. God values both you and the other person and wants each to move into maturity and responsibility. Paul boasts of his "authority for building you up rather than pulling you down, (and) I will not be ashamed of it" (2 Corinthians 10:8). When you confront someone who has violated your rights, think of it as assisting God in building their character as well as yours. This is part of your authority and is not something for which you need be ashamed.

On the other hand, if you are continually touchy and pride yourself on being "sensitive" and having a short fuse, perhaps you need to look at your excessive sensitivity in light of Christ's example. Orneriness and peevishness are not Christian virtues.

Recommended Activities

Examine Your Anger from a Spiritual Perspective

Make a list of the things over which you have felt anger recently. Reflect on these in light of the following questions:

- Are the things that anger you things that would have angered the Lord?
- Do the things you listed prevent you from doing God's will or being the person God wants you to be?
- Does every slight or irritation become a cause for you to count yourself or another out of the Kingdom?
- When you find that you have sinned with anger, do you quickly go to your sister, brother, or neighbor and make amends?

After you have reflected on the above, commit ways of dealing with anger to the Lord. Ask Him to teach you to express all of your emotions honestly and effectively.

Look to the Psalms for Ways to Express Anger

Find a Psalm where David or others express anger over a hurt or another's behavior. Note the passages where they tell God what they'd like to see happen to these enemies. Then see how they resolve or move beyond the anger to a place of worship and trust in the Lord.

Supplement to Lesson 13

Power Under Control

"God takes care of those who take care of themselves!" Many quote this most decidedly non-biblical saying as scripture when they are rationalizing aggressive behavior. While it sounds good on the surface, it overlooks God's preference for the poor, the powerless, and the oppressed. Spiritually speaking, one doesn't really come to the place of dependence on God until one reaches the limits of self-sufficiency. And yet, "If you belong to Christ, then you are Abraham's offspring, heirs according to promise" (Galatians 3:29). "You are a chosen race, a royal priesthood, a holy nation, a people for God's own possession" (1 Peter 2:9). As a son or daughter of the King, you are entitled to all the rights and benefits of royalty.

While the kind of leadership demonstrated by Christ was one of the suffering servant, it was in no sense that of the long-suffering door mat. Nor was it that of the self-effacing, toady, or prudent coward. There was nobility in Jesus even as He went to the cross. Never was He a victim. Even when He was mistreated, His meekness was actually *power under control*.

In the same way, the redeemed have God-given rights and powers which are available to them. You are somebody! In developing your assertive skills, you are taking hold of the power that is part of your inheritance in Christ. At times, it may be that for the sake of the kingdom you choose not to assert these rights. But as we saw in Lesson 11, God cares about your wants and needs.

He also cares about the person who you may feel is violating your rights. Who knows, you just might be God's instrument for calling this person to accountability or limiting the hurt this person can cause in others. Something else to consider is that hurtful behaviors may be due to the other person feeling threatened. Use your prayer power to advantage here. Is there something frightening about the way you are presenting yourself to him or her? When you feel threatened or intimidated by someone, ask the Lord to give you *His* perspective along with the opportunity and the courage to confront this situation.

Kingdom-Purpose in Standing Up for Yourself

Learn to do good; seek justice, reprove the ruthless; defend the orphan, plead for the widow. Come now and let us reason together, says the Lord (Isaiah 1:17, 18).

Have you ever thought about yourself in the role of "Defender of the Downtrodden," "Reprover of the Ruthless," "Advocate of the Widow and Orphan" before? Where will you find a better place for learning how to live these roles than in the school of your own relationships? Don't neglect reasoning together—negotiating—when it is necessary.

In fallen humanity, it seems that everyone wants his or her way. This is impossible. So in order to resolve conflicts in the manner that God wants us to, servants of the Lord need to develop and use a wide range of skills. This takes time, patience and listening as one sorts out what is needed, wanted, and acceptable to everyone involved.

When Jesus recited the summary of godly ethics, "You shall love the Lord your God with all your heart, and with all your soul, and with all your mind, and with all your strength...And you shall love your neighbor *as yourself*" (Deuteronomy 6:5; Leviticus 19:18; Mark 12:30, 31; etc.), He gave us permission to love and value ourselves. More than that, this ancient formula, the *Shema*, shows that we cannot separate love of God and love of neighbor from love of ourselves. As you learn to stand up for yourself, consider it practice for the future Kingdom assignments God may bring your way that will allow you to act as an advocate for someone without power.

As we mature in faith, we grow in the capacity to stand up for ourselves, others, and for God.

Recommended Activities

Review Your Assertiveness Skills

Make a prayer list of those situations where you feel you need to be more assertive. Who are the people involved? Using the "hands down, hands up" prayer attitude presented in Lesson 10, describe these to the Lord. Then, turning your hands up, give them to Him and wait to receive His insight, instruction, and peace for this process.

Make a list of people you know who seem to be able to appropriately express their needs, wants, dislikes, and limits. Pray thankfully for them and their example. Think of how you might let them know what their behavior models for you. You might ask them what motivates or frees them to be assertive or how they learned to know their needs and limits. You may be surprised to know that most people must learn these skills—they seldom just come naturally.

Plan an "assertive event." Practice stating clearly what you want or need. Imagine what the other person might say back to you and how you would listen carefully to this person's needs. Think of how you might negotiate so that both of you emerge with the feeling that you are winners.

Find a way that you can be an advocate for someone who needs *your* power. Many churches have groups or ministries to help the homeless, unwed mothers, refugees, abused children, or the elderly. Habitat for Humanity builds and refurbishes homes for people who would never be able to own one without volunteers like you to help with the labor. Maybe you could simply write a letter to a newspaper or public official expressing your concern about some issue. Make a plan to defend, to reprove, to come along side someone else as a daughter or son of the King.

Supplement to Lesson 14

Remember Whose You Are

People frequently mistake *meek*ness, which we defined in the last lesson as "power under control," for *weak*ness. "Humility and gentleness, with patience, showing forbearance to one another in love," is the picture in Ephesians 4:2 of Christian courtesy which accompanies meekness. And to some both in and outside the community of faith, it might seem like an invitation to resistance or manipulation.

It is in those encounters where your growing self-esteem and determination to live as a prince or princess of the Kingdom is put to the test. Among the basic ideas of The Path to Freedom on page iii are: "As each day passes, I am better able to think rationally and realistically, to look at life as a series of choices that God wants me to make as one created in His image with free will, and to stop and look before choosing."

We Christians sometimes try to take an easy-out saying, "I just want to do God's will," and then we sit and wait for Him to write on the wall. We forget that within the will of God is much permission. We have *free* will, which means He gives us *real* choices. As said before, we are not in an elimination game. God is not trying to trip us up and count us out. We are held securely by the love of Christ. Like children learning to walk, even our faltering steps are welcomed as we move towards wholeness in Him.

How we react to conflict is a choice allowed by free will. Therefore, we need to be competent in all of the basic approaches to conflict resolution—assertive, non-assertive, and aggressive approaches—so they are all options for us.

Carrying Your Banners Into The Battle

When our five sons were young, we would send them out the door saying, *"Remember whose you are!"* At first, they thought we were talking about belonging to my husband and me. Later, they began to understand that they were property of the Lord, created by Him, and redeemed by Christ's blood. This became one of my own "banners," under which I travel and under which decisions are made: I try to always be aware of Whose I am.

Another banner I raise when I have a difficult choice to make is the question: *"What is best for the Kingdom?"* Is this a time when I should be assertive, conform, withdraw, select a substitute goal, or be aggressive? How will it benefit the Lord, me, and the other person if I use this approach? Is this person's aggressiveness or resistance an unpleasant and habitual tactic for getting his or her own way? Or, is this a departure which signals a need for better listening or more compassion on my part?

You might want to adopt these banners. "Remember whose you are" reminds you that you are both beloved and a representative of the Lord Jesus Christ. "What is best for the Kingdom?" calls you to a higher purpose as you consider the immediate needs or wants of all who are affected. A third banner you may want to add is *"Practice the presence of the Lord"*, which is meant to reflect that almost automatic tendency to pray whenever you are making a decision, feel anxious or threatened. Silently, without anyone being aware of it, you can pray something like, "Lord, help me to understand what this person is saying. Why do I feel thwarted or threatened? What tactic is this person using? How should I respond?"

When Another Believer Sins Against You

Often our faith and confidence is tested in recurring conflicts with other Christians. These trials threaten our confidence and even our faith. Jesus was aware that these problems would arise within the church. He gave us a procedure to follow when we feel we have been sinned against by another in the community of faith:

> If your brother (or sister) sins against you, go and reprove him in private; if he listens to you, you have won your brother. But if he does not listen to you, take one or two more with you, so that by the mouth of...witnesses every fact may be confirmed. And if he refuses to listen to them, tell it to the church; and if he refuses to listen even to the church, let him be to you as (an outsider) (Matthew 18:15-17).

This formula usually is necessary only in those rare and extreme cases involving specific sin which goes unresolved and continues to hurt both individuals and the fellowship of the church. Most problems between believers can be settled quickly with some honest communication and perhaps negotiation, using the same skills one uses at work, home, or elsewhere. The less time that passes and the fewer people involved, the sooner most disagreements are settled.

Members of Christ's family have two other resources. In every church there are mature and caring people who can be called upon to help settle disputes. These arbitrators may be clergy, elders, deacons, or others with gifts of wisdom. Of course, the most effective Mediator is Jesus Christ whose Spirit is always accessible in prayer where two or three are gathered to genuinely seek His will.

The hallmark of the Christian community is that we are to be a people "diligent to preserve the unity of the Spirit in the bond of peace" (Ephesians 4:3). Indeed, the last prayer of the Lord with His disciples before He went to the cross was for love between believers which would demonstrate their unity.

"As a result (of our life in the body of Christ), we are no longer to be children...but speaking the truth in love, we are to grow up in all aspects...according to the proper working of each individual part, (thereby) causing the growth of the body for the building up of itself in love" (Ephesians 4:14-16). This is not a "peace at any price" kind of unity but one in which loving honesty provides growth for all.

Responding to Unsatisfactory Merchandise or Poor Service

What about those people we deal with who might not share our Kingdom values? What if we are treated unfairly in the marketplace? Since we are called to be good stewards, it is our responsibility to see that we receive value for value. Because we understand that all that we have is a trust from the Lord, it is important not to waste our resources. Insisting on satisfactory goods is also a way to learn to stand up for yourself. It is relatively safe to practice skills when you are dealing with someone who is not part of your every day life, and perhaps whom you will not have to see again, unless you choose to.

You will be more comfortable addressing poor service if you develop the habit of *commending* good service. Instead of saying, "Hey, you!", read the waiter's or waitress's name tag or ask. Practice treating all with whom you deal as persons loved by God, deserving the courtesy and dignity that you yourself like. But then, that is what real assertiveness is, isn't it?

Recommended Activities

Develop A Strong Belief In Your Right To Be An Assertive Christian

List all of the biblical reasons for standing up for yourself mentioned in this lesson. Include any others you might think of. Entitle this list, *I THINK GOD WANTS ME TO LEARN TO STAND UP FOR MYSELF BECAUSE...* Share these ideas with someone you trust, inviting them to add to them.

Practice Being Assertive In The Marketplace

As you wait to order, to pay your bill, or stand in line, pray for those who serve you. Think about what you would do if you were given the wrong order, bill, or if someone treated you rudely. What are your choices as a Christian?

Supplement 15 Lesson

Continuing Your Growth

You have come to the final lesson in your program but certainly not to the end of your journey with the Lord towards wholeness or holiness. If possible, set aside a full day or more of solitude. Go to a retreat center, library, quiet park, the country, or a garden to reflect on the last few months. During this time you can pray, read your journal, and record your progress and needs.

The key concepts in the *Spiritual Guide* are reflected in the scriptures chosen for each lesson. Take time to reread each of these verses and write your reflections in your journal. Compare your initial responses with what you wrote now.

It is my sincere prayer that you have established a firm habit of taking time alone with the Lord that includes meditation, prayer, and journal keeping. If not, I again recommend it. The spiritual disciplines are central to the Christian life. There is a large library of materials available under the general heading of "Christian Spirituality" or "Disciplines." The disciplines are like the training of an athlete. They make us fit for the contests of life and give us stamina.

The practices of seeking and giving spiritual guidance which have been maintained for centuries by the mystics and the religious in the Roman Catholic and Eastern Orthodox traditions have been rediscovered by Protestants as well. Your support person may also be a "soul friend" who encourages you in your relationship with God. Or you may want to begin looking for someone who will meet with you occasionally to share your reflections on your life and spiritual growth.

The disciplines should be called "the blessings," for what might have begun as mere duty or ritual, soon becomes a sanctuary of peace in our lives.

Sabbath rest is both a state of salvation and a loving provision from the Lord. It is not to be a work we perform to gain merit from God. Sabbath is a gift of repose that restores our energy and intimacy with the Lord.

A word of caution in the midst of promoting the disciplines of faith: guard against this becoming another avenue for the tendency towards perfectionism. Instead of demanding instant perfection in this or any area, seek to progress and increase those disciplines which enhance your life. Consider that over the life of the church few have had the luxury of owning a copy of the Bible or enjoying time to pour over it. And yet, this doesn't limit God's ability to communicate with and bring to maturity people in all circumstances. We need to guard against turning practices intended to bring us close to God into opportunities for "point-making," guilt-owning, ritualism, or perfectionism.

Like sabbath rest, this should be done in the manner of receiving a gift instead of working for God's (or other's) approval. In Jesus, we have all the religious ritual and all the righteousness necessary for acceptance by the Father.

>...if you confess with your mouth Jesus as Lord and believe in your heart that God raised Him from the dead, you shall be saved; for with the heart man believes, resulting in righteousness, and with the mouth he confesses, resulting in salvation (Romans 10:9, 10).

Have you done this? If not, take time right now to pray the "A, B, Cs of Salvation":

A: Admit that you need a *Savior*, that without God's help you are unable to deliver yourself from sin and those habits that would destroy you or others;
B: Believe that Jesus Christ died and rose again to deliver you from sin and death;
C: Confess with your mouth that He has done this for *you* and that you accept Him as your personal Savior and the Lord of your life. Receive His Spirit as His indwelling Presence in your life.

Now, rejoice that you are in the process of being saved. As John says, "It has not appeared as yet what we shall be. We know that, when He appears, we shall be like Him just as He is" (1 John 3:2). Enjoy your resulting righteousness, based not on your own merit or perfection, but on that of the Lord Jesus Christ.

Recommended Reading

Books on Biblical Concepts

Brueggemman, Walter. *The Message of the Psalms*. Minneapolis: Augsburg Pub., 1984.

Edwards, Gene. *A Tale of Three Kings: A Study in Brokenness*. Augusta: Christian Books, 1980.

Green, Michael. *I Believe in Satan's Downfall*. Grand Rapids: William B. Eerdmans Pub., 1975.

Green, Michael. *I Believe in the Holy Spirit*. Grand Rapids: William B. Eerdmans Pub., 1975

Books on Improving Relationships

Smedes, Lewis B. *Caring & Commitment*. New York: Harper & Row, 1988.

Smedes, Lewis B. *Forgive and Forget*. New York: Harper & Row, 1981.

Wangerin, Walter, Jr. *As for Me and My House*. Nashville: Thomas Nelson Pub. 1987.

Books on Self Examination

Hart, Archibald. *Adrenalin and Stress*. Waco: Word Publishing, 1986.

O'Conner, Elizabeth. *Our Many Selves: A Handbook for Self-Discovery*. New York: Harper & Row, 1971.

Smedes, Lewis B. *Choices: Making right Decisions in a Complex World*. New York: Harper & Row, 1986.

Yancy, Phillip and Brands, Paul. *Fearfully & Wonderfully Made*. Grand Rapids: Zondervan, 1987.

Books on Depression and Discouragement

Glaphre. *When the Pieces Don't Fit God Makes the Difference*. Grand Rapids: Zondervan Pub., 1984.

Greist, John H. and Jefferson, James W. *Depression and its Treatment*. Washington: American Psychiatric Press, Inc., 1981.

Nouwen, Henri J. M. *The Wounded Healer: Ministry in Contemporary Society*. Garden City: Doubleday, 1972.

O'Connor, Elizabeth. *Cry Pain, Cry Hope*. New York: Harper & Row, 1988.

White, John. *Putting the Soul Back In Psychology*. Downers Grove: Intervarsity, 1987.

White, John. *The Masks of Melancholy*. Downers Growve: InterVarsity Press, 1982.

Yancy, Phillip. *Disappointment With God*. Grand Rapids: Zondervan, 1987.

Books on Spiritual Growth

Bonhoeffer, Dietrich. *Life Together*. New York: Harper & Row, 1954.

Edwards, Tilden. *Spiritual Friend: Reclaiming the Gift of Spiritual Direction*. New York: Paulist Press, 1980.

Foster, Richard J. *Celebration of Discipline: The Path to Spiritual Growth, Revised Edition.* San Francisco: Harper and Row, 1988.
Guelich, Robert and Hagberg, Janet. *The Critical Journey: Stages in the Life of Faith.* Waco: Word Books, 1989.
Merton, Thomas. *Seeds of Contemplation.* New York: New Directions Pub., 1949.
Merton, Thomas. *The Seven Storey Mountain.* New York: Harcourt, Brace and Co., 1948.
Nouwen, Henri J. M. *Reaching Out: The Three Movements of the Spiritual Life.* Garden City: Doubleday, 1975.
Ogilvie, Lloyd John. *Praying With Power.* Ventura: Regal Books, 1983
Weavings, A Journal of the Christian Spiritual Life. Nashville: The Upper Room, bimonthly.

Books about Adventurous Living for Children of All Ages

Lewis, C. S. *The Chronicles of Narnia (Seven Volumnes).* New York: Macmillan Pub., 1950.
Wiederkehr, Macrina. *A Tree Full of Angels: Seeing the Holy in the Ordinary.* San Francisco: Harper & Row, 1988.

Index

Abraham (55)
Accepting questionable sources (21)
Adequate servanthood (26-27)
All-or-nothing thinking (20)
Anger (51-53)
    & sin (52-53)
Anxiety
    & faith (1-5)
    & negative anticipation (29-30)
Approval (33-36)
    & comparisons (49)
    & labeling (20)
    & personal worth (47-48), (56)
Assertiveness (53), (55-61)
    & injustice (56), (57)
    & meekness (55), (59)
    Resolving conflicts (60)
Body as a machine (7)
Born again (16)
Commitments (49)
Comparisons (49)
Compliments (48) (61)
Conflict, *see assertiveness*
Coping self-statements (9-10)
Creation (2)
    see also Fall
David (9), (20), (33-34)
Demons (v)
Discernment (21)
Distorted thinking (16), (19-23)
Distraction (11), (40)
Elijah (22)
Emotional reasoning (22)
Emotions (22), (51)
Fall, the (2-3), (5), (47)
Fleshly nature (6)
Fortune telling (21)
Free will (2), (59-60)
Guilt (23)
In vivo exposure (40-41)

Injustice (3), (15), (17), (31)
see also assertiveness
Jacob (39)
Jeremiah (9)
Job (22)
Joseph (15-17)
Judas (30)
Labeling (20)
Limitation
    & fleshly nature (6)
Magnification/minimization (21)
Meekness (55), (59)
Mind reading (21)
Negative anticipation (29)
Negative self-talk (9)
Overgeneralization (20)
Perfectionism (25-27)
    & spiritual disciplines (63)
Personalization (23)
Positive self-talk (34)
Redemption (13), (17)
Renewing of your mind (16)
Responsibility (2), (23), (30-31)
Sabath rest (11-13)
Salvation issues (20), (64)
see also redemption
see also transformation
Saul (33-34)
Should/must thinking (19)
Sin (30-31)
s. against you (60-61)
& anger (52-53)
Spiritual disciplines (63-64)
see also sabbath rest
Spiritual gifts (27)
Suffering, *see injustice*
see also, Fall
The Fall, *see Fall*
Transformation (16), (43-44)
Worship (39)

Bible References

Genesis
  1-3 (2)
  2:16, 17 (19)
  3 (3)
  3:1-4 (22)
  3:3-24 (3)
  37, 39-50 (15)
  39:20 (18)
  42:24 (16)
  43:30 (16)
  46:29 (16)
  45:7, 8 (16)
  45 (18)
  50,20 (16)
Exodus
  20:8-10 (11)
  20:11 (12)
Leviticus
  19:18 (56)
Deuteronomy
  5:15 (12)
  6:5 (56)
  30:19,20 (18)
  30:19 (19)
1 Samuel
  18:16 (34)
2 Samuel
  14 (37)
1 Kings
  19:4-7 (22)
Job
  2:9 (22)
Psalms
  1:2, 3 (37)
  4:4 (52)
  23 (9)
  40:8 (35)
  42:4 (39)
  55 (37)
  139 (1), (4)
  139:14 (22)

Song of Songs
  5:2 (20)
Isaiah
  1:17, 18 (56)
  2:3 (39)
  5:3-7 (31)
Jeremiah
  1:6-8 (9)
  1:6-7 (21)
Joel
  2:25 (48)
Matthew
  1:23 (30)
  5:17-48 (26), (28)
  5:48 (25)
  6:25-34 (32)
  6:31, 32 (29)
  11:29, 30 (42)
  18:15-17 (60)
  18:22 (20)
  28:10 (30)
Mark
  8:33 (52)
  12:30, 31 (56)
Luke
  6:26 (34)
  6:27 (34)
  10:42 (48)
  15:11-32 (49)
John
  1:47 (48)
  3:14, 15 (3)
  3 (16)
  5:6 (44)
  8:2-11 (52)
  8:31, 32 (19)
  8:44 (3)
  10:10 (3)
  14:30 (3)
  17:15 (v)
  21:15-17 (30)

Romans
  1:16, 17 (48)
  4:25 (31)
  5:3-5 (44)
  6:1-4 (6)
  7:15-25 (6)
  8:21, 22 (17)
  8:26-28 (17)
  8:28 (31)
  8:35-39 (30)
  10:9, 10 (64)
  12:18 (23)
  12:2 (43)
  12:3 (16), (23)
  12:3-8 (21), (24)
  14:13 (21)
  14:19 (21)
  16:1-12 (48)
1 Corinthians
  3:6 (49)
  4:3-5 (49)
  12 (21), (24)
  12:6 (27)
2 Corinthians
  3:18 (43)
  3:4-6 (26), (28)
  4:4 (3)
  5:17 (44)
  5:21 (31)
  7:5, 6 (5)
  10:8 (53)
Galatians
  1:10 (34)
  3:29 (55)
Ephesians
  4:2 (59)
  4:3 (61)
  4:11-16 (21), (24)
  4:14-16 (61)
  4:26 (52)
  6:11-18 (v)

Philippians
  2:12-13 (44)
  2:19-30 (48)
  4:4-7 (iv)
  4:8 (11)
2 Timothy
  2:15 (36)
  3:16 (v)
  4:17 (26)
Hebrews
  4:9-10 (12)
  4:12 (v)
  7:26 (31)
James
  4:7 (v)
1 Peter
  2:9 (55)
  5:6-10 (iv), (4)
  5:8a (36)
1 John
  3:2 (20), (64)
  3:2, 3 (26), (28)
Revelation
  3:20, 21 (47)
  12:9 (3)
  21:3, 4 (3)

Supplemental Materials

This book has been designed to be used in conjunction with *Anxiety, Phobias & Panic: Taking Charge and Conquering Fear*. Many people find these two books sufficient for their needs. However, others find one or more additional materials described below of great benefit.

ANXIETY, PHOBIAS & PANIC: Taking Charge and Conquering Fear

by Reneau Z. Peurifoy, M.A., M.F.C.C.

Designed as a series of fifteen easy-to-follow lessons, this books begins by answering the most commonly asked questions about anxiety. The lessons then describe how to use powerful cognitive and behavioral approaches to change the way you think, feel, and act. The book is full of practical exercises showing the reader how to apply the concepts and ideas it presents. Instructions for the exercises are given step-by-step in simple language.

The Relaxation Response Series

This series contains four programs on two audio cassette tapes. These programs help you develop cue-controlled relaxation—the ability to trigger the relaxation response by simply placing two fingers together. These programs also help make relaxed diaphragmatic breathing, externalization, and basic stress management skills automatic behaviors.

The Changing Attitudes Series

This series contains ten programs on five audio cassette tapes. These programs are designed to be used just before you go to sleep. They communicate directly to your subconscious mind and reinforce the information and skills presented in the lessons.

Taking Charge and Conquering Fear

On this set of eight audio cassette tapes you meet the author of *Anxiety, Phobias & Panic* as he talks about the ideas and skills presented in each of the lessons. It's almost like having Mr. Peurifoy right there with you. There are also interviews with people who have used the program successfully. The discussion tapes can be played while you drive, work, or relax. These programs are especially useful for people who find the material difficult, who learn best when information is explained verbally, or who just find it difficult to stick with a set of written lessons.

A Talk with Marjorie Working

On this set of two audio cassette tapes, Mrs. Working discusses the biblical principles she has written about in this book. The word of God comes alive as she speaks to you in her warm, personable style.

Price List

Individual Tapes (Two programs on each tape)

101 RR-1: Developing a Relaxation Response .... $ 9.95
    RR-2: Increased Relaxation with Relaxed Breathing

102 RR-3: Externalization 9.95
    RR-4: Increasing Your Stress Management Skills

103 CA-1: Replacing Should/Must Thinking With Positive Problem-Solving 9.95
    CA-2: Increasing Your Rational Self-Talk Skills

104 CA-3: Accepting Errors and Imperfection 9.95
    CA-4: Facing Life as a Positive Realist

105 CA-5: Approval 9.95
    CA-6: Self-Esteem and Self-Acceptance

106 CA-7: Transforming Anger into a Positive, Constructive Force 9.95
    CA-8: Releasing Resentments and Accepting Change

107 CA-9: Positive Assertiveness 9.95
    CA-10: Overcoming resistance from Others

Multiple Tape Sets

901 The Relaxation Response Series 17.95
    (all four Relaxation Response rograms on two cassettes)

902 The Changing Attitudes Series 41.95
    (all ten Changing Attitudes programs on five cassettes)

903 The Relaxation Response/Changing Attitudes Combinded Set 55.95
    (all Relaxation Response and changing attitude
    programs on seven cassettes)

904 Taking Charge and Conquering Fear 63.95
    (an individual discussion of each of the fifteen lessons in
    ANXIETY, PHOBIAS & PANIC plus interviews on eight cassettes)

905 The Complete Set 98.95
    all Relaxation Response, Changing Attitudes and Discussion programs on fifteen cassettes

906 A Talk with Marjorie Working 17.95
    (a discussion of the principles in A SPIRITUAL GUIDE on two cassettes
    **Special Offer: This set only costs $13.95 when purchased with
    any other cassette set**

Books

B05 Anxiety, Phobias & Panic: Taking Charge and Conquering Fear 12.95
B06 A Spiritual Guide Through Anxiety 6.95

Order Form

Name: _____

Street Address: _____

City: _____ State: _____ Zip: _____

Telephone: (___) _____

Please send the following:

Quantity	Item #	Description	Unit Price	Total Cost

Total Order	
California Residents Only Add 6.5% Sales Tax	
Shipping & Handling	
Grand total	

Shipping & Handling Charges

$0.00 - $9.99 = $1.50
$10.00 - $19.99 = $2.50
$20.00 - $29.99 = $3.50
$30.00 - $49.99 = $4.25
over $50.00 = $5.50

Add $3.00 for COD

Please make your check or money order payable to: LIFESKILLS

Mail your order to: LIFESKILLS
P.O. Box 7915
Citrus Heights, CA 95621-7915

sg